A Purple-Golden Renascence
of
Eden-Exalting Rainbows

A Purple-Golden Renascence
of
Eden-Exalting Rainbows

New and selected poems of

Hugo G. Walter

Fithian Press ❦ Santa Barbara, California ❦ 2001

PUBLISHED BY FITHIAN PRESS
A DIVISION OF DANIEL AND DANIEL, PUBLISHERS, INC.
POST OFFICE BOX 1525
SANTA BARBARA, CALIFORNIA 93102

LIBRARY OF CONGRESS CATALOGING-IN-PUBLICATION DATA
    Walter, Hugo, (date)
    A purple-golden renascence of Eden-exalting rainbows : new and selected poems / by
Hugo Walter
       p.   cm.
       ISBN 1-546474-378-0
       I. Title.
       PS3573.A472283 P87 2001
       811'.54—dc21   00-012690

CONTENTS

THE SPIRIT OF NATURE

OF DIVINE-GLOAMING WISDOM AND EDEN-EXALTING SPACES

THE SOUL OF THE UNIVERSE

THE SOUL OF THE TWILIGHT SEA

I am the soul of the asphodel-burgeoning universe
Permeating silver-lyred, jonquil-diffusing silences
Of Psyche-altared, nirvana-glistening light in amaranth-
Rising incarnations of moist-acanthus, Eleusinian-flowing,
Aegean-seminal dreams
I am the dusk-arching heart of the garden
Shaping chrysalis-lavender, Stygian-throned heavens
In Florentine-misting symmetries of orchid-plumed,
Empyrean-rippling moonlight
I am the spirit of divine light
Reclaiming the lily-gloaming heart of Blenheim-effulgent
Autumn from Ozymandias-cairned torrential-hours
Whispering poppy-meandering seeds of marble-pulsing,
Hopetoun-germinating evening in Venus-coursing
    absolutions
Of willow-emerald, fugal-pristine paradise
I am the soul of the twilight sea
Bearing marigold-prophetic chalices of calyx-floating
Stars and coral-enchanted smiles to the pearl-azure shore
Of sage-listening eternity shaping pyramid-scrolled cloud-
Haloes in grail-leavening tremors of Aeolian-saffron suns.

A Delphic-Winding Castle

I am the fertile-cairned, Redon-chrysalis silence
At the dahlia-globed heart of the orange-cypress-pinioned,
Pomegranate-confessing tree

A Corot-white castle of cyclamen-perpetual autumns
Shears the crimson-leavened twilight from convolvulus-
Requiemed skies into the mimosa-cavernous apparitions
Of its own Cecilia-enshrining heart

Crystalline-turquoise butterflies and Hesperus-rising masks
Of pearl-helixed wisdom seal chrysanthemum-ringed souls
In jade-melodic, Cybele-deepening reveries
Of Hohenschwangau-sceptered light

A Delphic-winding castle of red-gloaming dreams
Vanishes in the auburn-effulgent silence of its own
Perpetuity unseen by mortal eyes except when the amaranth-
Templed wind rustles golden-webbed whispers of ancient-
Hermetic horizons across Nolde-sacred vases of zinnia-
Diapason exultations

I am the Böcklin-wise, unicorn-serenading silence
Shaping heron-magenta, diva-pilastered estuary-essences
In Turner-prophetic diffusions of marble-chambered,
Mellifluous-yellow light.

I Am a Gobelin-Emerald Reverie

I am the saffron-lyred heart of the Nymphenburg-lavender
Stone shaping obelisk-singing, azalea-sweeping expanses
In celestial inclinations of Apollonian groves
Carving magnolia-enlightening, ivory-exalting truths
On grail-altared, forsythia-tinted auras of Tuscan-
Illimitable urns reshaping the garland-extending vista
Of merlin-shadowed, trefoil-cresting dreams in anemone-
Weaving, silver-misting Lucerne-silences
I am the Atlantis-liminal breath of the chandelier-
Germinating epiphany investing my soul in every other
Stone, the Beningbrough-permeating, jonquil-luminous spirit
Of the Arundel-perfecting isle of Cythere-embalming
Preludes, I am a Gobelin-emerald reverie of sublime-arching,
Cypress-templed timelessness redeeming mortality
In Ispahan-veined, magenta-rising transformations
Of twilight-saving, amber-gloaming stones infusing
Versailles-lambent, titan-amorphous synergies
With Meissen-crystalline, diamond-astered effusions
Of maroon-symphonic, Turner-effulgent light.

A GRAIL OF AUTUMN-SCEPTERED LIGHT

I am a vase of salmon-crescent, Adonis-effulgent light
Rising from the ocean in an auburn-chorused reverie
Of asphodel-awakening, Rodin-elegiac annunciations

I am a grail of autumn-sceptered light ascending
Vetheuil-animating marrows of sky where only tessera-
Pale albatrosses and pink-gelatinous pulsations conceive
Pristine-jade folds of amulet-trembling calyx-winds

I am a chalice of mimosa-silver, amaryllis-passionate
Light transforming hourglass rituals
To divine-murmuring, Elysian-tender silences
Transmuting ancient-tidal veils of nightingale-cradled
Truth to perennial-white, Eden-dewed stars

I am a constellation of pearl-engraving rains,
Shiva-melodious chasms, and muse-generating ballet-
    tempiettos
Dissolving the maenad-viscous flux of agaric-lithesome,
Arctic-manacled rivulets in the amber-ethereal,
Willow-intense depth of sunset-perfecting,
Cathedral-shaping prophesies of Promethean-misting,
Emerald-resonating light.

THE SOUL OF THE MANTLEPIECE

The Mansard-blue soul of the pomegranate-flourishing
Mantlepiece rises in marble-blossoming visions
Of diamond-lintelled solitude spreading ethereal-domed
Wisdom around the spacious-twilight chamber beyond
Triadic-virginal veils of ephemeral-mitred dust
The grail-sceptered soul of the Inveraray-timeless
Mantlepiece filling the andante-tapestried room
With the sunflower-lambent perfection of its inner
Illumination floating pyramid-extending shadows
Of immutable delight across my horizon-conceiving,
Rembrandt-liminal mind shaping the amaranth-sacred
Beauty of sapphire-redeeming rainbows and autumn-
Helixed silences in Eroica-unvanquished, heliotrope-
Gleaming synergies of Pythian-omnipotent innocence
And emerald-lyred, Michelangelo-gloaming omniscience.

I Am an Amber-Prophetic Stone

I am a madonna-wise piece of andante-liminal stone
Creating Gothic-torrential, Marmorsaal-radiant manor-
Aureoles consecrating silver-encircling silences
Of hyacinth-spiritual shadows in stained-glass triptychs
Of phoenix-empyrean mazes waiting for the melisma-
Spinning evening sun to touch zodiac-destined, wisteria-
Grottoed leaves around me in a crimson-apsed ferment
Of Peterhof-soaring solitudes

I am an amber-prophetic stone speaking in the dusk-
Gloaming tones of porcelain-twilight, sunflower-yearning
Paradise I am the Turner-eloquent soul of the jonquil-
Glorifying chandelier encompassing the sacred-
Illuminating profundity of the ancient-timbered,
Dynastic-proportioned aura in universe-spanning
Thresholds of Harlaxton-magnanimous, amaranth-
Effulgent space

I am an Amsterdam-vaned stone washed by nocturne-soft
Horizons sealing the reveries of the lotus-shaping moat
In crescent-dewed silhouettes of astral-corniced time
I am a diadem-templed stone breathing Elysian-tendrilled
Intimations of heliotrope-swirling light over the deluge-
Flickering fields and mandolin-cairned meadows
I am a Delft-pealing stone weaving the acropolis-saving
Silences of the asphodel-helixed wind in pomegranate-
Leavening mirrors of Ruisdael-lambent, acanthus-golden
   light.

THE SPIRIT OF THE PALLADIAN BRIDGE

I am the spirit of the Palladian bridge
Shaping Ionic-white, cedar-fluent passions
Of amaranth-sublime, acacia-cresting light
Across obelisk-blue pallors of Dardanelles-
Misting, hydrangea-sated memories

I am the spirit of the snow-meandering silence
Knowing that all will come to pass that is in the heart
In golden-veiled paroxysms as the Hermitage-vaned wind
Breathes amber-gloaming eaves of damask-prismed light
Across the green-listening, sapphire-inundating sea

I am the spirit of the Hyperion-consecrating court
Spreading the Handel-wise magnanimity of my soul
Into the jonquil-fermenting sky and the diamond-
Fusing horizon I am the harbinger of coniferous-
Eclectic dreams and sunset-secluding soliloquies

I am the diadem-apocalyptic blossom of lily-expanding
Life perpetuating helicon-lambent moor-silences
In wisteria-endless arabesques of saffron-concentric
Cloud-gladioli I am the Wilton-sealing destiny
Of threshold stones wandering in diastolic-orange,
Poppy-engraving mazes of twilight-pergola,
Orphic-soaring reveries.

THE WISDOM OF THE EVENING WIND

I am the magenta-crystalline silence of the forest lake
Suffusing Astarte-cairned tears of mortality
In turquoise-pealing, Geneva-sonorous incantations
Of hydrangea-exalting, Artemisian-pristine light

I am the ancient-helixed wisdom of the evening
Wind shaping hyacinth-astral augurs of Pythian-white
Timelessness across auburn-gentian, emerald-leavening
Horizons of Chartres-acanthus nocturnes

I am the amber-gloaming solitude of asphodel-evolving
Paradise transforming mistral-pallid memories
Of transience to Elysian-conceiving, cypress-streaming
Melodies of jonquil-refulgent, Rilke-iridescent
Immortality

I am the amaryllis-sighing dream of eternity
Whispering Ruisdael-lambent halos of golden-tendrilled
Light across willow-opulent meadows and anemone-
Effulgent spaces of the Apollonian-lyred heart
Of the universe.

OF TARANTELLA-APSED CLOUDS

The Halifax-polygonal streaming of tarantella-apsed clouds
Drips fragile-mazed trees of purple-luminescent,
Crepuscular-sage blooms and magenta-pellucid megaliths
Of orchid-golding light onto marble-silent, sphinx-
Panelled fields as a Castalian-lonely figure shapes
The evening-tremulous, Syon-dewed wind in jade-
   leavening,
Mandarin-enthroning hieroglyphs of honey-myrtle,
Pink-almandine light carving his astral-tendrilled,
Onyx-gloaming soul on dusk-timeless, Elysian-pulsing
Whispers of the calyx-chastening, pearl-discoursing sea
And on Neptune-templed truths of porcelain-epiphanic,
Minerva-pristine twilight.

THE SOUL OF THE DANCE I

I am the Nataraja-perpetual soul of the dance
Carving staccato-laminating embers of jasmine-
Subliminal rhythms on miranda-embracing melodies
Of Parthenon-white, damask-pure light

I am the muse-astered soul of the dance
Pulsing porcelain-vaned tremors of the dusk-
Lyred divinity across auburn-leavening
Convergences of diamond-lintelled, astral-
   germinating epiphanies

I am the Fauve-tendrilled soul
Of the dance saving the twilight ballet
Of the sea from sable-sirocco, Lethe-wreathed
Dreams floating gardenia-diapason, albemarle-
Ethereal radiances of amber-philomel, ancient-
Tiffany chalices in Elysian-prismed silences
Of golden-chrysalis, autumn-sapphire rainbows

I am the Nataraja-vaulting soul
Of the dance perpetuating Giverny-streaming,
Wisteria-glistening rituals of pomegranate-meadowed,
Sphinx-confessing eternity in mandala-soaring hearts
Of jonquil-diffusing, Aphrodite-helixed renascence.

I Am the Spirit of the Sunlight

I am the spirit of the hyacinth-singing sunlight
As it weaves Beauvais-sonorous fusions
Of golden-mullioned silences and jade-
Glistening horizons in heliotrope-unfinished
Distances of crimson-duned, pantheon-
Iridescent solitudes I am a Stourhead-conceiving
Reverie of jonquil-diffusing light fulfilling
The shape of the sea in the Aeolian-prophetic
Destiny of my amber-architraved, iris-evolving
Soul I am an amethyst-sacred temple of auburn-
Cascading light carving Endymion-pale inflections
Of astral-wayward immortality on Salisbury-lichened
Agoras of chrysalis-corniced squalls in magenta-
Inventing, lilac-symphonic gardens.

OF CHARTRES-OGIVAL SOLITUDES

I listen to the chrysalis-ranging, purple-oracular
Leaves speaking of Chartres-ogival, marble-sentient
Solitudes at the Atlas-stamened edge of the crimson-
Angular, iris-deepening abyss

I listen to the white-mullioned tremors of the alpine-
Inviolable, hyacinth-streaming sky shaping the lily-
Winding ease of pyramidal-vermilion intuitions
Of hermetic-golden, Murillo-soaring light

I listen to the Couperin-fragrant leaves revealing
The orphic-magenta soul of the crystalline-sage,
Aeolian-lyred horizon in salmon-cresting, hydrangea-
Glistening soliloquies of jasmine-ethereal,
Isis-enchanting convolvulus-shades

I carve astral-labyrinthine omens of dusk-orange
Temple-orchids on mantra-effusive, velvet-chasmed
Etudes of ancient-vernal, asphodel-iridescent seas
As the amaranth-leavening wind seals andante-
Effervescent aureoles of Turner-melodic, forsythia-
Pealing timelessness in bronze-prismed, poppy-
Effulgent courtyards.

MARIGOLD-GERMINATING CHALICES

Marigold-germinating chalices of light
Rise from the hydrangea-sacred pond
In auburn-gentian entropies of primrose-
Masked shadows as the alabaster-leavening cascade
Seals dusks of timelessness in hyacinth-embering
Silences of chrysalis-jade, orchid-weaving dreams

Rose-architraved, lavender-saffron fragrances
Of diamond-breathing light drip mellifluous-astered
Melodies from Delphic-maned clouds in seraphic-vined
Synergies of silver-auguring, pomegranate-marrowed truths

Amber-soft angels ripple across clover-mullioned pools
Of gladiolus-soaring light in polyphonic-yellow
Valences of cypress-opulent rhythms as the ancestral-
Pinioned call of the golden-necked swan converges
Saffron-diaphanous, Poseidon-mazed voices
In fern-pealing, amaryllis-streaming grails
Of magenta-ringed, asphodel-deepening light.

In Moss-Helixed Synergies

I am the Dionysian-martyred soul of the convolvulus-
shoaled
Mausoleum shaping primordial-auburn blooms of allegretto-
Paned light in Monticello-pulsing expanses of crystalline-
Mazed solitudes

I hear the orange-diapason voices of Bernini-sceptered
Prophesies a thousand miles beyond the edge of time
And yet within the inner resonances, forever permeating
The crimson-stamened, Memnon-garlanding echoes
Of my diastolic-veined, magenta-nomadic soul

I am the marble-gentian spirit of Ascott-conjuring
Amplitudes of sapphic-holy, renaissance-conceiving light
Dissolving time in moss-helixed, cyclamen-vaulting
synergies
Of Michelangelo-gloaming, rainbow-intense stones

I see the Aphrodite-lambent eyes of mantra-dewed,
Poinsettia-soaring immortality in sapphire-
Haloed tears of Promethean-lyred pallors
I feel the nocturne-splintering, anemone-widening
harmonies
Of the architectonic-misting horizon in the marigold-
Arching wombs of my silver-incarnate, vernal-perfecting
soul

I am a spherical-latticed odyssey of wisteria-morphine,
Jade-iridescent silences of a hundred Sevres-lavender
Mandalas waiting to be reborn in Florentine-wise cascades
Of grail-leavening suns transforming poplar-scented veils
Into orphic-almandine breaths of Castle Howard-exalting,
Tiffany-Elysian light.

Across the Sea of Galilee

I spill luminous whispers of time across the sea of Galilee
Coral-turquoise dusks of time transmuting
Rainbow-swelling winds in altar-splaying fingers of
    onyx-pale light
Seeking lavender arbors of architrave-languishing truths,

I weave Babel silences of Vienna-blue communion gardens
In velvet-purple euphonies of motionless, precipitous
    mill-echoes,
Twilight adorations of immaculate silver breezes
Seeking blue-neon crosses of Eden-phosphorescent stars

In silent eaves of ineradicable faith and bronze-foam
    rosaries,
Epitaphs of ancient souls in cyclamen mirrors
Of Artemis-wandering dawns, seeking internal harmonies
In chrysalis-ascending nocturnes of Lindisfarne-amaryllis
Dreams.

I OPENED A STAR

I opened a star
And found a piece of time
A piece of orange-helixed time
A foundling piece of time
Lost by Mercury, dispersed by Minerva,
Forgotten by God—waiting for the sea,
Waiting for fragile-listening epitaphs of frost-shafted
    horizons,
Waiting for mandrake-dusk elixirs of salmon-columbine
    light;

I opened a star and found
A piece of cyclamen-lavishing time,
Of calyx-chastening, solstice-surging time
Diffusing light in Magdalene carnation-arpeggios,
A piece of morning spinning summer ivories
Of words in moon-compassed pools of amphibrach lilies
Suspending light in orphic-trellised, harp-satyred
    dominions;

I opened a star
And found a piece of time
Along the Sargasso edge of lavender-madrigal twilight
Lost from chamomile-lace wings of soft-gusting angels
Shaping Babel crocuses into soft-broken, maroon-thistled
Silhouettes of saffron-desolate tears,
A piece of endless, gelatinous, immortal time
Waiting for prophesies of sunflower dreams,
Healing fissures of auroral-lemon silences.

Shaping the Figures of the Dance

A dance of twelve crystalline-jasmine waves across the
 platinum-lambent shore of eternity
A dance of twelve Sidha karya offerings across an iris-
 consecrating lake of fallow lightning
A dance of twelve violins across an allegretto-discoursing
 pastiche of sforzando-pendulous unicorns
A dance of twelve snapdragons across a translucent chime
 of palomar-garlanding light
A dance of twelve breezes across a crimson-diapason
 meadow of Florentine-onyx oases
A dance of twelve Artemisian-lavender, Eroica-
 perpetuating lines sheltering the green-apsed, mirabelle-
 chastening divine eye
I am the Degas-calligraphic, solstice-winding soul
 of the universe shaping the figures of the dance
  in lotus-furrowed mirrors of grail-sceptered
   silences and tiffany-amber suns.

The Silence of Autumn

I am the saffron-lambent, vermilion-architraved silence
Of autumn shaping seraphic-astered tremors of Knole-
Eaved, hyacinth-longing eternity in the amber-haloed
Breaths of the Apollonian-helixed, emerald-pealing
Evening wind

I am the Delphic-mazed silence of Artemisian-liminal
    dawns
Pulsing diamond-leavening, grail-refulgent melodies
Of golden-mullioned, asphodel-vaned timelessness
Across bronze-pyred, jonquil-burgeoning meadows
Of amaryllis-dewed, crimson-adamanthine light

I am the silence of the yellow-sentient leaves falling
On the cypress-veined stones in soft, warm breaths
Of the evening sun as the wind of Indian summer
    perpetuates
The Catskill-ethereal loneliness of wisteria-lambent,
Maple-hallowed solitudes of marigold-breathing light

I am the lilac-paned, amulet-iridescent spirit of the autumn
Graveyard evolving the apricot-effulgent spaciousness
Of the sacred grove in ancient-cairned, andromeda-
    lithesome
Silences of camellia-astered, Parthenon-marrowed leaves.

A Salmon-Shadowed Figure

A salmon-shadowed figure entering the mist-leavening,
Fjord-softening waters of the talisman-margined forest-lake
Ascending the threshold aura of the divine
In his own damask-serene, porcelain-templed mind
Moving on mandala-dewed tremors towards the
  adamanthine-
Crimson, saffron-gloaming source of Pythian-oak,
Cypress-embering sublimity, an orphic-halcyon creator
Shaping abbey-crystalline scansions and legato-eternal
Silences of the dusk-blooming horizon in pristine-
Luminous solitudes of moist-cisalpine infinity;

A phoenix-conceiving creator among his catacomb-staved
Moor-chimes carving dove-Cistercian knells of amber-
Rolling Pleiades on autumn-aspen monoliths of pandora-
Spectral arias, filling promontory spells
With sandstone epitaphs of dactylic-liminal light
Breaking fragile-emerald mirrors of time on willow-
Splashing vagaries of Rehoboth-hieratic barrow-dreams,
A silmarillion-serene composer shaping Rhadamanthus
Absolutions from tidal wisps of summer-amoebae dreams
Calling crescent-counterpaned, dawn-veined clouds
Into august-lavender lagoons of calyx-cascading,
Maple-webbed light
Calling the sea home to his Thames-silent, moss-
Cadenced shore of twilight immortality.

31

PILASTERS OF SOFT-DEWED OMNIPOTENCE

As the Scythian-majestic towers rise through the Maia-
Empyrean mists the silence of the apocalypse peals
Across the sable-merlined wind the moss-darkened clouds
Reappear and disperse in crimson-apertured cycles
Like Gunterstein-furrowing thoughts in linden-silver
Panoplies of moor-gleaming, auburn-chasmed light
Corinthian-pinioned pilasters of soft-dewed omnipotence
Surging through amorphous-duned blizzards of white-
    cairned
Breezes shaping immaculate-jade dreams of golden-veined
Pallors on onyx-lonely bridges of Palladian-wise intensity
Two figures sharing contemplative, mercurial radiances
With cypress-cascading horizons touching the sun
Through the amber-knolled haze in amethyst-enamelled
Pyres of orange-diapason light carving the madrigal-
Pristine aura of apricot-divine timelessness
On crocus-glistening melodies of Brussels-golden
Synergies as diamond-lintelled meridian-stars conceive
The oracular destiny of the magenta-effusive sky
In lavender-architraved billows of Geneva-equinoctial,
Fountains-whispering light the sea becomes a dusk-
Crystalline incantation of azalea-translucent,
Tiffany-astered chandeliers reshaping the sun
In chartreuse-tendrilled, burgundy-acanthus altars
Of lily-gloaming, amaranth-centering light.

ACROSS ARCADIAN MEADOWS

When a silent-sublime creator walks across
Arcadian-liminal meadows of marble-gentian light
She lures perpetual-sage time away from mortality
And shapes transience into russet-steepled mists
Of immutable-soaring skylarks and eglantine-fervent,
    muse-blossoming paradise

When an amaranth-floating creator permeates the sky
With cypress-roaming solitudes and emerald-adamanthine
Chimes of Hermes-shadowed towers he opens the
    translucent
Folds of eternity in saffron-gloaming epiphanies
Of cosmic-pensive, willow-germinating paean-harmonies;

An orphic-chrysalis heart of sapphire-liberating,
Helicon-preserving vales and Byzantine-resonant,
Ambrosial-articulate magnanimity shaping tiara-poised
Silhouettes of time in lavender-infallible, madrigal-
Glowing silences emanating from porcelain-meadowed,
Crimson-ripening light-vases,
A divine-conceiving heart of Parnassus-revolving
Harmonies guiding lost souls to lily-cascading, azure-
Binding sanctuaries of Gautama-burgeoning, emerald-
    feeling
Light.

The Soul of the Dance II

We are the soul of the dance
In hexagonal-coloratura symmetries
   of magenta-silicon mezzotints
We are the Shiva-culminating soul
Of the dance in melisma-curving
    nebulae of jasmine-cresting,
      panorama-mazed wisdom
We are the soul of the dance
In supple-aquamarine fantasies
   of auroral-descending light
We are the soul of eternity shaping
The willow-pulsing horizon
   in Tchaikovsky-vaned synergies of light

We are the soul of the dance
In dynastic-silken rhythms of marigold-
Christening radiances we are the soul of the dance
In Michelangelo-gloaming, andante-flowing waves
Of chiaroscuro-leavening, albemarle-deepening light
We are the soul of the dance in lily-
    cascading, porcelain-ripening cadences
      of orphic-resurrecting, cypress-spanning
        Artemisian mysteries

We are the soul of the twilight-breathing wind
Healing the mistral-glazed wounds of mortality
In azure-masqued, anemone-luminescent silences
   Of Promethean-lyred, acanthus-concentric
     Emanations reuniting Adonis-lingering,
       Lily-pulsating intuitions with the crescent-
Sage, divine-opalescent dawn of eternity

A DANCE OF TWELVE SOULS

A dance of twelve goldenrod-tasseled trees
    along a palomar-divine lake of Aeolian-raising
      purple-thistle-lulls

A dance of twelve loggia-bells on a chamomile-
    pervading sea of Aphrodite-crimson light

A dance of twelve Olana-sunset silences
    on a Pleiades-marble reverie of willow-profound,
      Isis-shrining cloud-truths

A dance of twelve serpentine-weaving shadows
    along a heath-misting path of Matterhorn-lonely,
      maze-astered head-stones

A dance of twelve mandrake-converting exiles
    of cruciform-sage, Promethean-spiring light

A dance of twelve myrrh-solemn portals
    around a genesis-revealing, grail-sacred apotheosis
      of cypress-winding, dusk-autumn light

A dance of twelve orchid-winds across an Iris-
    architraved meadow of petunia-alabaster,
      apricot-rhythmed light

A dance of twelve orange-topaz day-lilies
    before the mosaic-singing, aquamarine-
      transmuting apocalypse

A dance of twelve crystalline-pallid whirlpools
of megalithic-arching light on andromeda-
porcelain hexagons of russet-yellow-undulating
infinity

A dance of twelve souls of Apollonian magnanimity
given freely, joyously, lovingly
to a world wrapped in intolerant imperfections

A dance of twelve Gautama-spacious souls
of rainbow-surging, Rembrandt-veined melodies
transmuting time in amber-gyred affinities
of resonant-yellow, onyx-diagonal reflections

A dance of twelve pomegranate-horizoned soul-voices
shaping the Adriatic-runed edge of time
in philomel-intuitions and anemone-encompassing
sighs of Easter-stamened, Ravenna-moist solitudes

WHEN THE TIDE RISES

When the tide rises on a vortex of light
The sea becomes an amaryllis-helixed blossom
Of sphinx-tendrilled anemone-tears conceiving
The hydrangea-spacious radiance at the iris-
Lyred heart of the universe
A Venus-pale figure rises from the chrysanthemum-
Apsed marrow of moist-stone demoiselles haunted
by ruby-cascading vagaries of Watteau-plumed
Solitudes when the honeysuckle-almandine sky
Congeals in a fleur-de-lys-ivied seraph
Of sepulchral-wise asphodels an arpeggio-golden moon
Drinks the shadows of the apocalypse in azure-harped
Flames of Florentine jeunesse becoming a mistral-
Dewed reverie of auburn-gloaming light as Beatrice
Walks across purple-lambent waves towards
The deluge-sealing, amethyst-engraving
Isle of twilight.

THE GARDEN OF THE LILY

I wander through the mahogany-paneled, gavotte-
   primordial
Corridors of auburn-globed silences and tiara-endless
Pallors coming into the Garden of the Lily
Who welcomes me radiating cedar-pale chasms
of amber-gelatinous dreams into my soul
Smiling a crocus-rapturing flame of love at me while
Turning into a pomegranate-sceptered, arabesque-
Translucent eye as she weaves her astral-tendrilled,
Anemone-widening reveries into my spirit and washes upon
The shore an emerald-lambent grave of galactic-pearl,
Seine-dewed light I look into the nocturne-fermenting
Depths of her onyx-beige eyes and become a sapphic-holy,
Chrysalis-floating elixir of acanthus-furrowed, maroon-
Symphonic shadows I wade into the sea of her soul
With marigold-pilastered intuitions of tempest-driven,
Primrose-leavening solitudes as the dusk-germinating wind
Echoes orphic-contoured sadnesses across cyclamen-
   confessing,
Mandala-encompassing horizons of almandine-embering,
   Melpomene-
Eglantine light.

A Solitary Figure

An Arcadian-solitary figure listening to the primordial
Concurrence of the evening waves, watching the
  crystalline-
Panelling horizon shape mosaic-sapphire tonal-mists
Into hieratic-white epochs of grail-resplendent amplitudes
And megalithic-yellow Kandinsky-silences,

A Delphic-solitary figure along mangrove-jade interludes
Of heron-magenta light and kithara-nesting seagull-
Destinies walking into dune-astered, Balmoral-pure
Thresholds of anemone-burgeoning, auburn-rhapsodic light,

A mauve-saturated unity of emerald-vaned metamorphoses
Along the dusk-anvilled shore listening to the mirabelle-
Sublime presence of bronze-gloaming, damask-nocturne
Solitudes and the aureole-whispering, Rembrandt-amaryllis
Chimes of eternity.

THE BEGINNING OF IMMORTAL WISDOM

The marble-anemone glistening of the Pleiades-amber
Evening sun on the jade-redeeming waves is the beginning
Of immortal wisdom

The emerald-chastening solitude of the lagoon
Is a primrose-leavening garden of divine-rippling
Whispers of white-absolving, Atlantis-liminal light

The amaryllis-breathing, mandolin-swelling silence
Of the Castalian-rhythmed shore is the rainbow-
Sharing, eglantine-prophetic resonance of crystalline-
Twilight eternity

When the vermilion-spherical waves rush across
The dusk-framing heart of the paradise-refining
Pool the world-soul trembles cypress-winding, lavender-
Moist reveries of sapphire-gladiolus, asphodel-
Burgeoning light

As alabaster-ecstatic rivulets of an Eleusinian-flowing
Timelessness and dune-astered paeans of dithyrambic-
Lucid solitudes shape the immanence of auburn-mazed,
Pearl-soaring crests of horizon-spanning light
In azalea-sentient, ambrosia-lintelled waves
Of acacia-numinous, Poseidon-conceiving cloud-helixes.

THE NOCTURNE OF ETERNITY

Let the Raby-amber solitude weave jonquil-mazed
Silences into ambrosia-veined rainbows of melisma-
Orange, helicon-fermenting dreams as the Palmer-saffron,
Astral-vaned clouds shape purple-lichened shadows
Into sapphire-gleaming, solstice-ringed apparitions
    of delight
Let the hyacinth-dewed, virginal-masked reveries
Of spectral, symphonic gazes discern the columbine-
Majestic silhouettes of the divine in Jungfrau-misting,
Stygian-lambent euphonies and Salisbury-primeval
Whispers of golden-canticled, Minerva-effusive light
Let the Floors-astered tranquillity of Protean-effulgent
Sympathies conceive the burgundy-haloed, lavender-
Breathing nocturne of eternity in almandine-echoing,
Dahlia-embalming mirabelles of asphodel-consecrating,
Ivory-sibylline, lemon-lazuli light.

WHEN TWILIGHT FALLS

When twilight falls along the shore
The seagulls cry against the waves
Nirvana parables of eternity
Cytherean whispers of forgotten graves

When darkness talks to silver-vertigo sands
Of Nietzsche and de Chirico
Phoenix-jade echoes swelling soft-crepuscular bands
Of onyx-bridled anemone dreams across

The journey of the old magi
Still travelling, drifting in time
Still searching for a lost omen
Of wisdom, a saffron-veined rosary of light,

When twilight falls against the edge
Of an old tavern, no one is there—
An agony of emptiness spills
Over her auburn-scattered hair.

The Dream of the Waterfall

I listen to the dream of the waterfall
Splashing from magenta-apsed, Baltic-pealing silences
To dusk-architraved, astral-veined amplitudes
Perpetuating a reverence for life
In amaryllis-nocturne, onyx-deepening melodies
Of auburn-madrigal, Orpheus-pulsing light

I listen to the Eroica-mazed resonances of the diamond-
Sparkling sea sealing time in wisteria-dewed cascades
Of jade-astered, azalea-trembling light as the ambrosia-
Leavening wind shapes palomar-christened, lapis lazuli-
Expanding horizon-aureoles into asphodel-soaring,
Lotus-altared grails of saffron-healing,
Monet-crystalline light

I listen to the crimson-pinioned, apocalypse-
Scented silences of the emerald-diapason, moon-
Saturated millennium weaving Caspian-tendrilled,
    camellia-
Streaming intimations of Magritte-liminal, crepuscular-
Lambent light in Cythere-almandine, marigold-lintelled
Blossoms and mandarin-pink, lilac-compassionate whispers
Of cypress-germinating, seraphic-luminescent rainbows.

In Isis-Weaving Temples

A figure dancing the ritual of life
In purple-ancestral waves of cherry-trancing blossoms
Converting arcade-silent fears and odyssey-divine tears
To prodigal-lonely dusks of poppy-red promises
A figure dancing the destiny of love
In Isis-weaving temples of palomar-christening lace
Transmuting flamingo-raging storms of sibylline mirrors
To silver-crescent synergies of carmine-misting light
A figure carving the color of joy
On the muse of the spheres
Infusing her crystalline-lambent, Hera-magenta soul
With arabesque-vermilion tremors of dominion-
Awakening eternity saving lunar-gelatinous Montmartre-
    pools
In pearl-conjuring revelations of Diana-luminous, vestal-
    streaming eyes.

THE SPIRIT OF STONY BROOK BRIDGE

The Spirit of Stony Brook bridge
Glistening in russet-saffron dawns
Of emerald-gray stones
Hovers over me gently, stealthily
In a fine mist of jade-lavender whispers
Wondering if his stones are as old
As the stones of Monte Cassino, Chorin Cloister,
The ruins of Tintern Abbey, or
The bridge over the Delaware;
The Spirit of Stony Brook bridge
Flowing in alluvial wails
And twilight arpeggios of crescent-ochre spells
Flowing in perpetual silences of lost evenings
Flowing in autumnal tympanums of sibylline counterpanes,
Wondering if his stones are as old
As the sun, wondering if his stream is
As old as time.

DUSK-MARTYRED HARMONIES

Toccata-amber, Chartres-cochineal aureole-silences
Permeate clerestory-radiating, empyrean-tidal
Amplitudes of crimson-fugal, stone-weaving light
As the Gothic-sceptered, auburn-germinating vortex
Scatters orange-diapason, sable-glistening organ-tremors
Of saffron-marble, wine-stamened eternity and pink-
Astered poinsettia-pulsations of seraphic-crystalline,
Magenta-pealing light across pristine-medieval
Solitudes of acanthus-violet stained-glass paradise,
Dusk-martyred harmonies generating the salvation
Of timelessness as Christ rises in bronze-pyred,
Aeolian-profound exultations of hermetic-golden,
Maroon-ethereal light.

GAZELLE-WHITE CYLINDERS

Gazelle-white cylinders of asphodel-pure light
Gather crystalline-eaved intuitions of fritillaria-
Murmuring, dusk-scented equinoxes along the emerald-
Diffusing edge of the crescent-madrigal, acanthus-
Golden rainbow as the evening sea pulses providence-
Swelling winds into Aegean-amaryllis gardens
Of maroon-sepulchral, primrose-enchanted light
Promethean-spired steps floating lavender-silken
Tendrils of muse-whispering calyx-webs
In auburn-lyred, fugal-evergreen
Silences of perpetual-sage,
Mount Stuart-exalting light.

A MARBLE-LAMBENT STATUE

A marble-lambent statue in the loggia-ancient courtyard
Embalmed in sapphire-adamanthine streams of cherry-
   vaned,
Dawn-leavening blossoms creating crimson-architraved,
Jade-helixed prophesies of diastolic-orange, lemon-apostolic
Horizons from azalea-exalting breaths of ruby-paned
Reflections shaping damask-prismed veils of Kinross-astered
Timelessness in Parnassus-apsed memories of melodious-
Cairned, primrose-fermenting stones, an emerald-archetypal
Statue converging the magenta-pallid voices of the
   apocalypse
In chrysalis-dewed soliloquies of Paris-radiant
Circles of Hyperion-vaulting, wisteria-sealing light,
An onyx-tendrilled statue evolving the pristine-refulgent
Rhythms of the helicon-angled dawn in amaranth-
   glistening
Calligraphies of Rodin-sceptered, phoenix-chanting light.

THE ISENHEIM ALTARPIECE

Until the world understands the Isenheim Altarpiece
Nothing will change,
A crucifixion of hermetically painful silences and coronal
Dawns weeping seeds of panhellenic graces
Bearing the sins of the earth in pearl-stained tears
Of extraterrestrial wisdom, bearing the hope of the earth
In horizon-rainbow apostrophes of ancient-alluvial
    adorations,
The face of Rembrandt knows the immortality of sunflowers
In the solstice-ascending radiance of Atlantis-astered
    dreams
A timeless face of ethereally lonely wisdom
Only when Rembrandt shows Christ the sunflowers
The Chartres-empyrean, self-surpassing radiance
Of Van Gogh's flowers in endless saffron-stamened
Synergies of amaranth-helixed light
Will the seraphic-crystalline river of polyphonic
Diffusions begin to flow in odyssey-surging, toccata-
Amber echoes along the immortal edge of the Isenheim
    Altarpiece.

THE EVENING CLOUDS

The gondola-reticulating clouds are the Cisalpine-
Endless, Newstead-exiled thoughts of a divine mind
Searching for the leviathan repose of tameless,
    Praxiteles tears,
The Hesperus-expressing clouds are the last mural-
Adoring reflections of a messiah-protean mind
Recasting its immortality in vermilion-webbed,
Stratus-astered vortices of myrrh-glowing light
Sealing its Olympus-sheaved link with the sun
In an auburn-crystalline, Cyclades-converging beam
Of sublime-abalone, pearl-eaved silences,
Dark-foaled tempietto-megaliths on the Nepal-
Twilight horizon congealing ancient wind-echoes
In labyrinthine-trembling mirrors of amber-
Dewed, silver-breathing light.

AN ORANGE-DRYADIC SUN

An orange-dryadic sun thickens acacia memories
    Of light across arborealis silhouettes of time
As the ritual of life swelters in diastolic echoes
    Of decaying Mediterranean sands, waiting for the gust
    of wind
Coming out of a crystalline-primeval window-pane
    Scattering frail, everlasting presentiments of wisdom,

Of the wisdom of evanescence, into the universal
    Night of the soul, I condense time into thresholds
Of light, where the sea haunts the dawn
    In soft-lacquering haloes of pomegranate and
Jade absolutions, only the maroon-diffusing sunset

Reveals the truth about the Amber-misting horizon
    In cinnabar-dewed, camellia-soaring
Rhythms of hyacinth-veiled,
    Golden-fevered altars.

I AM THE SAFFRON-MELISMA SILENCE

I am the saffron-melisma silence of the ageratum-dewed
Morning sun shaping the spirit of the primrose-radiating
Meadow in hydrangea-vaned streams of emerald-astered
    light
In cerulean-veined wisps of Pissarro-effulgent delight
I am the soft-lyred, gladiolus-burgeoning diaspora
Of the Minerva-ethereal sun creating the poppy-magenta
Heart of the marigold-helixed universe in astral-
Germinating mandolin-reveries of anemone-crystalline,
Lavender-mazed light
I am the honeysuckle-lambent silence of the Apollonian-
Pristine sun sealing the eternal spirit of the jonquil-
Stamened clouds in delphinium-arbored chalice-dreams
Of Chatsworth-vaulting horizons in willow-soaring
    amplitudes
Of diamond-architraved light
I am the marble-gelatinous silence of the Lennoxlove-
Refulgent sun carving ancient-trellised soliloquies
Of the palomar-isled divine on auburn-glistening waves
Of jasmine-whorled seas pulsing amaryllis-pealing paeans
Of wisteria-helixed light towards the Aeolian-seraphic,
Damask-prismed shore of asphodel-murmuring,
Orpheus-sceptered eternity.

Perfecting the Wisdom of Immortality

In the lotus-iridescent, silver-venerable morning light
A Vishnu-breathing, Athena-numinous figure raises
The rainbow-scrolled altar of a sacred-luminous,
Heaven-evolving grove along a sapphire-passionate river
At the primrose-astral edge of eternity
Perfecting the wisdom of immortality
In Ragley-blossoming auras of divine-vaulting,
Marigold-primordial silences carving amaranth-
Lintelled, dahlia-pulsing incarnations on mirabelle-
Chiming, sutra-vaned pillars of onyx-flowing, Bernini-
Sceptered light shaping the magnolia-supple, Elysian-
Lambent truth of the dawn in damask-immaculate,
    camellia-
Mandolin arbors of lily-diapason, Cythere-streaming,
Saffron-consecrating light.

EROICA-MODULATING EPIPHANIES

Revelations of an Indus-whispering mind
Beyond basilica-mazed stone-rituals
And Byzantine-dusted sunset-meridians embracing
The Isis-deepening universe of dahlia-globed
Masks and poppy-murmuring light at the threshold
Of the brine-molten, compass-gleaning horizon
A Shiva-tidal incarnation of the spirit
Beyond time and history culminating in the flamingo-
Confessing wisdom of angelus-transmuting light
A mind of Thoth-dewed clouds
And coreopsis-germinating helixes
Of amber-tendering light which changes
And reshapes itself but cannot die
Transforming mortality into Eroica-modulating
Epiphanies of night-dissolving, marsh-
Golding grace, timeless chiaroscuro-effusions
Of windmill-evolving, saffron-asphodel light,
A mind shaping its spiritual permanence
In the aura of sublime-terraced autumn-icons
Of crystalline-surging, Delphic-eaved sunset-moors
And iris-vaulting, Drumthwacket-sage harmonies
Of the fermata-ribboned, crimson-vespered west wind.

THE ANGELS OF THE ANNUNCIATION

The angels of the annunciation
Only reappear when the amaranth-blue,
Chrysanthemum-consecrating wind rustles softly
Through immaculate-jade, porcelain-blossoming birches
And when dusk-perfecting, menhir-lambent aureoles
Of late-afternoon wind-knells convene
The Mnemosyne-tenoned renascence of acacia-
Numinous, pine-sceptered silences,
The angels recasting time
In El Greco-luminous calligraphies
Of lily-arching, rune-chasmed voices
And dithyrambic-willow dreams of amethyst-hexagonal,
Piranesi-spiraling domes of liminal-apertured light,
Saffron-rising, Delft-winged angels reshaping
Empyrean intuitions of ineffable, Bernini-agape
Joy in the auburn-delicate, pomegranate-scented
Opulence of the nativity and in unicorn-sheaved
Prisms of orchid-weaving, amber-purifying timelessness.

SAVING THE DREAMS OF HERMES

There was a traveler on the silent road
Who walked alone for Atlas-dewed, acacia-endless
Miles where few would dare to tread and weep
He walked away inevitably from the lichen-darkened
Vanities and sable-masked corruptions of civilized
Illusions to the sacred forest where a lapis lazuli-
Haunted, marble-ringed castle lay upon the primeval
Heart of Nature, he strode through the laurel-
Darkening hallows of time-fettered vapors where
Only calico-ewered carrion and red-shrouded ghosts
Rise from the mistral air, they touched him not,
They let him pass as if they knew of his coming,
As if his presence were foreordained by raven-
Billowing silences, as if a spectacle of amber-
Furrowed flames illumined his inner way, the lonely
Traveler came upon the castle with the mantra-chiming,
Janus-labyrinthine door exuding pale-golden phantasma
Of philomel-mourning moor-gleams, he became a Lethe-
Sceptered resonance of diamond-effulgent light saving
The dreams of the horizon in willow-lingering chalices
Of sublime-pulsing tempests in his equinoctial-serene
Castle saving the dreams of Osiris, Athena, and Hermes
In the wreath-templed glooms and alabaster-mazed reveries
Of his Titian-effusive heart—once every thousand years
A solitary traveler knows the road to eternity
In the Salisbury-emerald profundity of his damask-
Shattered, saffron-germinating, agape-flowing soul.

OF AMSTEL-VANED SOLITUDES

In the pomegranate-dewed, ethereal-gray shadow
Of the estuary-veined windmill rises a margrave-solstice
Figure endowed with Elysian-tendrilled eternity
By amber-kinetic blooms of ancient-Bavo winds and blue-
Tempest peals of Catskill-spiring willow-truths
Dispersing Promethean-tessera hymns of architectonic-
Primeval isolation, untouched by Taormina-fertile
Rivulets of vain, hourglass rituals, creating the pyramid-
Sage sublimity of sail-dissolving, saffron-tremulous
Timelessness in Hyperion-discoursing silences of cobalt-
Mediating, Amstel-vaned solitudes.

THE POEM

The poem is a fragile silence
Where the sky meets the sea
In an enchanted moment
Of ethereal dreams and unvanquished epiphanies,

The poem is a soft-amber vision
Of pallid, pendulous augurs of eternity,
A sanctuary of self-overcoming Promethean rituals,
An immortal wound of Apollonian light,

The poem is a place where the poet
Can breathe freely, fully,
And search for truth and faith
Vitally beyond mortality;

The poem is a voice seething broken-chiming
Rivulets of Munch echoes across dusk-sibilant margins
Of alabaster-phoenix, Goya-solstice dreams,

A voice beyond aberrant-apsed amplitudes
And sinewy-promising sabbaths, lifting
The sea from soft-embered estuaries

Of prodigal time, a voice transmuting seasons
Into inviolate insinuations of pyramid-dawns
And helix-running sand-graces,

A voice beyond the remembrance of time
Beyond chrysalis-surpassing knells, a voice
Calling quietly in sapphire-palladium repose.

A MIST OF MARIGOLD-INTUITIVE COMMUNIONS

When the moon shapes the heart of the cypress
In magenta-veined blooms of light a double rainbow
Rises from the sea in Cythere-streaming reflections
Of Pleiades-amber suns and eglantine-prophetic resonances
Of lilac-permeating, Cassandra-evolving wisdom
A primrose-leavening deluge of angel-traversing light
Opens the stone-lichened doors of the ancient temple
Closed for centuries an acacia-numinous mist of marigold-
Intuitive communions creates the Atlantis-liminal soul
Of the Castalian-rhythmed horizon in mandrake-gloaming,
Eleusinian-flowing diasporas of pink-amaryllis, Delphic-
Weaving eternities.

A Millennial-Sacred Grove

A millennial-sacred grove where the Florentine-magenta
Confluence of the light of four porcelain-sage vases
Is the emerald-astered soul of eternity

A vase of gladiolus-conceiving, purple-iridescent muses
Receding into dove-interminable distances of pallid-
Glowing, Renoir-immaculate silences

A vase of piazza-feverish solitudes decaying into orange-
Metaphysical shells of crystalline-fertile, Fontainebleau-
Exalting light

A vase of Vermeer-listening mirrors arching into
Petrified-combing obelisks of Cassandra-elegant shadows

A vase of diachronic-lemon astral-harps animating
The sea in amphora-infinite mobiles of sphinx-hermetic,
Lunar-weeping light

A sacred-lavender grove where the diffusion of the light
Of melancholy-jade haloes of cypress-germinating,
Dusk-embalming statues is the renascence-breathing soul
Of Blickling-effulgent eternity.

I Am a Goldau-Misting Tapestry

I am a Goldau-misting, Eastnor-sacred tapestry
Of unicorn-dreaming, Elysian-tendrilled snow-aureoles
Shaping the first day of spring in cypress-radiant
Cantatas of pearl-shadowed, onyx-soaring synergies
Sealing the flux of time in phoenix-dewed silences
Of Lyndhurst-exalting, velvet-trembling light
I am the hyacinth-weaving, amaranth-diapason heart
Of the Gobelin-streaming, Pythian-veined wind
Carving apocalyptic-jade blossoms of magenta-perfecting
Genesis on amaryllis-chiming, marble-gloaming mirrors.

Self-Transformation

I waited by the sea for the apparition
To emerge from heliotrope-magenta waves
I waited to behold the golden-dewed chalice
In his turquoise-ewered hands
And as he came upon the shore
The waves drove tempestuous-lintelled cries
Across the sands towards emerald-sated skies
And as he held the Hever-vestal chalice
Over the Aeolian-moist reveries an auburn-
Tendrilled sunset-gleam arose from indigo-
Spectral clouds to pierce the shining vortex
And as they touched the old world ceased to be
A deluge of crimson-mantled, cedar-haloed light
Vanquished the semblance of a world and created
A new arabesque-conceiving tapestry of life
The apparition became the new sun and I became
The sea along the amaranth-templed shore where
Penshurst-arching silences share onyx-scrolled
Divinations of sacred time with melancholy-
Raptured sighs of seagull-wandering, iris-yearning
Solitudes and the chalice became the mantra-pulsing
Horizon where sibylline-veiled eternity meets
The Arcadian-possessing pause of Pleiades-curving
Infinity.

I Am the Rubens-Panelled Soul

In the azalea-vaulted corridors of the east cloister
Linger marble-veined memories of ancient-madrigal silences
A Tudor-domed mantlepiece of rainbow-persisting
   arabesques
Exudes hyacinth-parabled, Vishnu-apsed voices
Of oaken-pilastered, Hesperus-lyred dreams
Rose-trellised crosses perceive the seraphic-misting flux
Of the sable-cairned dance in Vesuvius-rustling flames
Of mandrake-dewed, golden-diaphanous elixirs
I am the Rubens-panelled, porcelain-blossoming soul
Of the zephyr-carving, astral-dawning gallery
Restoring the vermilion-architraved, obelia-murmuring
Euphonies of the gargantuan-chasmed manorial halls
In ruby-astered effusions of Buckingham-jonquil light
In auburn-elusive incarnations of Blenheim-ethereal,
Fugal-pristine mirrors.

THE APOLLONIAN-SAGE BRIDGE

I am the voice of the Mozart-soaring light
Shaping chamomile-leavening, acropolis-veined petals
Into almandine-eclectic suns of Michelangelo-gloaming
    eternity

I am the silence of the Grieg-misting darkness
Shaping cairn-willowed eaves of tiara-masked
Radiances into Böcklin-mitred isles of Hades-astered moons

I am the veil of the Picasso-horizoned morning
Transforming crimson-globed spaces of lavender-
Vestal light into Isis-effulgent melodies
Of poppy-weaving, amber-helixed dreams

I am the jonquil-ringed, Apollonian-sage bridge
Of Rhadamanthus-echoing, emerald-pilastered
Twilight connecting life and death in pink-
Ethereal, Elysian-tendrilled seas of Beethoven-
Luminescent, lily-diapason cherry blossoms.

IN DELPHIC-PURE INTIMATIONS

I am the damask-liminal heart of the Antwerp-sacred
Stone shaping the adamanthine-yellow tears
Of the universe in the Elysian-tendrilled depths
Of my apocalyptic-wise, auburn-diastolic soul

I am a crimson-architraved chalice purifying
The light of mortality in the pristine-ethereal
Solitudes of my Sevres-almandine, chrysanthemum-
Streaming spirit as the evening wind shapes cobalt-pink
Arabesques of gladiolus-vined mirabelles in the sunset-
Diffusing mists of Ispahan-lacquered, jade-astral
Dreams

I am the sibylline-fragile, amber-trembling source
Of the wisteria-glistening, carmine-fountained horizon
Beyond stranded boats and desolate rocks enshrining
The autumn-lambent wisdom of the cumulus-burgeoning,
Cassandra-pulsing universe in the violin-cascading
Melancholy of porcelain-marrowed, nightingale-
Turquoise silences

I am the orange-asphodel-conceiving,
Pink-jonquil-emanating heart of the Tiffany-mazed,
Lily-gloaming garden shaping the sunflower-exalting
Threshold of eternity in Delphic-pure intimations
Of Wilton-effulgent, iris-deepening dreams.

A Dunrobin-Vaned Blossom

I am an iris-lambent, Dunrobin-vaned blossom
  of forsythia-saving dusks reshaping the light
    in amber-streaming melodies of Apollonian-sage
      dreams

I am a lavender-enchanted blossom of lily-golden
  light leading souls across the Gothic-liminal bridge
    between life and death embracing solstice souls
      in damask-eaved euphonies of willow-murmuring
        aureoles

I am a crimson-architraved chime of light guiding souls
  across the waterfall of emerald-opalescent time
    to primrose-amphora meadows of silver-helixed
      delight

I am a Hera-magenta breath of anemone-engraving wind
  perpetuating hydrangea-resplendent adorations
    of dune-scented evening in diamond-immaculate
      silences of saffron-diapason light.

PRESERVING THE HEART OF THE UNIVERSE

I walk through the ancient-calypso cemetery
In Kandinsky-almandine reflections of twilight-
Consecrating silences listening to the voices
Of lichen-engraving stones speaking of dusk-
Orange blooms of gladiolus-soaring light
Listening to the voices of tempest-lacquered
Tantra-chalices speaking of the divinely pure-
White heart of Apollonian-profound cloud-dreams
Listening to the voices of the evening sea
Shaping the emerald-generating apertures
Of a Cyclades-traversing temple along the deluge-
      sceptered, tiara-misting shore

I walk through the clouds in apocalyptic homage
To Sistine-galactic solitudes whispering yellow-
Tonal auras of timelessness to passing meteors
Of purple-angular light shaping frescoes
Of hibiscus-concentric reveries on synthetic-
Webbed, Munch-tentacled aspirations
Of crystalline-moist moon-dances
Preserving the heart of the universe
In the saffron-gloaming streams, symphonic-
Lavender aureoles, and chrysalis-mazed, cypress-
Diastolic harmonic-visions of my light-conceiving,
      sunset-redeeming soul.

THE SOUL OF THE UNIVERSE

I am the soul of the universe
Collecting Gautama-fragile sadnesses in my soul
Gathering Pythian-white clouds of melancholy
Sagacity in the dusk-compassionate expanse
Of my Vedic-whispering soul
Shaping the hope of the world
In amber-gloaming, acacia-numinous timelessnesses
Of my Bernini-sceptered, lily-conceiving soul
Perpetuating Snowdonia-cresting, delphinium-
Frescoed resonances of saffron-evolving, azure-
Unvanquished trinities of Aphrodite-shrining light

I am the soul of the universe
Integrating divine-opalescent angles of sea-composing
Harmonies with muse-weaving calyxes
Of late-afternoon, millenial-astered horizons
Pervading the Thoth-sheaved longevity
Of alchemistic meridians with chrysalis-luminescent
Tonalities of pine-cosmic evening-silences
Shaping the Giverny-flowing, wisteria-lavender
Timelessness of pristine-adamanthine forests
In Promethean-sage, amaryllis-halcyon reveries
Of orchid-twilight memories of Friedrich-altared,
Magenta-soaring eternity

I am the soul of the universe
Consecrating cyclical convergences of camellia-
Blossoming, Jura-trembling thresholds
In Geneva-columbine incantations of Florentine-
Vaulting, Elysian-perfecting cloud-hearts
Revealing rainbow-diastolic, Apollonian-pure
Diffusions of the sublime-luminescent, helicon-
Serene soul of Nature

I am the soul of the universe
Saving autumnal-megalithic suns and ancient-
Madrigal moons from the whirlpools of time
In Arlington-effulgent dawns of my diamond-
Lintelled, marigold-diapason soul
Embracing the soul of the sea
With mimosa-helixed, sapphire-iridescent sunset-winds
Of my amaranth-resurrecting, Orpheus-pulsing soul.

THE SPIRIT OF NATURE

THE MORNING DEW IS A DANCE OF DIVINE WHISPERS

The morning dew is a dance of divine whispers
Shaping the first surf-tendrilled, Pleiades-surmising
Waves of Artemisian-lavender, gladiolus-soaring light
In miramar-venerating, cypress-floating reveries
Of dahlia-luminescent, mandala-pervading eyes

The morning dew is a purple-misting tarantella
Of mountain-swirling light shaping the auburn-
Crystalline sea in sundial-mahogany preludes
Of azalea-refulgent incantations in aquamarine-
Liminal nocturnes of Matisse-pink-discoursing
Horizon-mirrors

The morning dew is a red-globed oasis
Of salmon-androgynous, delta-winged silences
Conceiving sapphire-lambent, asphodel-pure synergies
Of Aurora-sophic, silken-altared omens and lilac-
Sparkling, Orangerie-sunset ballerinas.

THE THRESHOLD-WIND

In the lavender-onyx rustling of the late-afternoon
Threshold-wind I hear ancient-Ganges soliloquies
Of hydrangea-blue, sapphire-meridian light shaping
Thames-burgeoning annunciations of saffron-diapason,
Ring-corniced light in porcelain-templed
Calligraphies of luminous-helixed wisdom

In the mandala-leavening threshold-wind
I hear Stygian-white prayers of the Protean divine
Spilling pink-tempera suns across Amen-martyred
Refractions of Nile-auburn light murmuring nightingale-
Architectonic prophesies of Athena-wandering dreams
On delta-marlin covenants of galvanic-altared sand-dews

In the amaranth-moist threshold-wind I touch the
    Apollonian-
Crimson, muse-weaving source of poetry, of all eternal-
Shrouded, poinsettia-scrolled words, and alcaic-
Extraterrestrial voices in silver-oracular, Rhine-deepening
Reflections of divine-crepuscular, marble-surging silences

The dusk-tempest threshold-wind reveals the angel-healing,
Marigold-communing secrets of the myrtle-blessed,
    palladium-
Megalithic bridge in Michelangelo-incarnate breaths
Of tidal-infusing beings creating the mosaic-spinning
Soul of the paradise-confessing universe from oasis-pristine
Aureoles of Aegean-amaryllis, conch-ribboned light.

The Pool of Water Lilies

The empyrean-solitary pool of water lilies above time
Floating marigold-lyred aureoles over diastolic-trembling
Labyrinths beyond dawn-sceptered knells of cerulean-jade
Oracles and silicon-sunset silences of Vedic-warm rainbows
Beyond Hera-magenta arbors of delta-winged larkspur
And crescent-blue, Alhambra-misting iris-valences
Cassandra-evolving, oasis-embalming visions of
    diaphanous-
Pearl echoes spawning pink-anemone, palladium-soft
    breaths
Of Delphic-pulsing timelessness across millenial-epiphanic
Suspensions of marble-streaming, Pachelbel-dewed
    horizons;

The Meissen-crystalline pool of water lilies beyond fragile
Chimeras of time, creating its own coronal apex
Of Rembrandt-veined light transforming the sun and god
Into amaryllis-incandescent swallows of Promethean-amber
Light shaping Orangerie memories in garland-glowing,
    dove-
Whispering helixes of saffron-consecrating light and rosary-
Tendrilled, mosaic-auroral chimes of Giverny-permeating,
Bronze-gloaming mirrors.

AN AMETHYST-GLISTENING PETAL

The gray-whispering, amber-veined clouds have a profound
Wisdom said the northern wind far beyond that of the
    pallid-blue heavens
A wisdom of sibyl-converging stones preserving heliotrope-
Mazed visions of damask-silvering eternity

The majestic-blue, topaz-radiant clouds have a supreme
Wisdom said the southern wind far beyond that of the
    alabaster-gray endlessness
A wisdom of sea-inventing, turquoise-architraved
Echoes of cedar-permeating eternity

Only the amaranth-crystalline light of the Pythian-
    listening,
Carnation-weaving evening knows the truth as it shapes
Sunset-tympani in Nolde-gloaming helixes of candelabra-
    magenta melodies;

The clouds smiled upon me in their marble-effulgent,
Pastel-galactic magnanimity lifting my soul
Into their hibiscus-expanding, lapis lazuli-conceiving
Mists where I saw the mandrake-confessing, iris-brooding
Gardens of eternity illuminating the Harlaxton-towering
Dome of heaven, in the emerald-singing, chrysanthemum-
Glowing silences I heard asphodel-pulsing reveries
Of lily-germinating, Turner-iridescent light
I became an amethyst-glistening petal of the Hesperus-
Eloquent cloud-heart floating on Isis-cascading
Intuitions of Aegean-discovering, Atlantis-divining light.

THE SOUL OF THE LAKE

On a moist-purple, sun-shrining July morning
He understood the soul of the lake
As he gazed into the dark green-pervading silences
He understood in his innermost soul
The Chopin-pristine language of the windswept ripples
As he sat in melancholy loneliness along the reed-misting
Banks his soul became one with the willow-sentient
Waves with the ribbon-flowing geese
With the purple-languid rushes with the amaranth-
Leavening soul of the divine pool
Crystalline-jade ripples perpetuating the lotus-
Radiant permanence of their own incarnate
Profundity, he spoke to the waves softly
And the waves spoke back caressingly
Sharing their genesis-persistent wisdom of immortality
With a nature-prophet bound to the deluge-
Nurtured beauty of their perpetual-listening silences
And then the breeze ceased and the lake
Became as clear as jasmine-diaphanous harmony-glass
In the depth of the waters he saw
In a Minerva-pallid mirror the soul of the lake
Shaping timeless rhythms of Gemini-green light
In a Beethoven-liminal epiphany of asphodel-blossoming,
Emerald-lyred beauty he saw the lily-vaned
Silences of his own soul.

Twilight Invocations of Dusk-Mourning Beauty

Let the soul of the sea shape your soul
In Castalian-blossoming tremors of silver-
Crystalline eternity in the aura of gladiolus-
Perpetuating, mural-seraphic silences
The clocks are transmuted into crimson-effulgent
Chalices of Etretat-blue light

Let the soul of the sky shape your soul
In Andes-streaming reflections of jade-haunted
Moons in the aura of lighthouse-Nepenthe reveries
The pendulums are transformed into mountain-liberating
Angels converging softly in the alcaic-vaulting
Hearts of lily-onyx suns

Let the soul of the earth shape your soul
In Renoir-vermilion trilogies of rose-cream ripples
Existing only for the sensuousness of their own
Inner light in the aura of Luxor-burgeoning
Modulations apocalyptic-tensile rhythms fade
Into lapis lazuli-breathing, poppy-veined mirrors
Of rainbow-tentacled, Orangerie-sunset light

Let the soul of the divine shape your soul
In Chartres-enchanted nocturnes of Psyche-fevered,
Amaryllis-glistening light in the aura of Thames-
Echoing twilight-invocations of dusk-mourning beauty
The hourglasses vanish in Venus-sapphire chimes
Of Norham-pristine, nightingale-hermetic light.

THE VOICE OF ETERNITY

The wind is the Woburn-immaculate voice of eternity
Casting dune-fountained visions of margrave-wandering
Souls onto sea-leavened canvases of Byzantine-tessera
Horizons as a solitary figure gathers helicon-pulsing
Sheaves of dusk-golden light in his cinnabar-glowing
Hands and in the Aegean-moist corners of his mind
Shaping them into nirvana-gloaming whispers
And albemarle-gesturing shadows of arborealis-chastening
   cloud-haloes
A daily absolution of chiaroscuro-rising, spire-
Reincarnating energy of the ancient-martyred,
Palladian-wise self,
A transformation of the cumulus-mazed self
Into sulphurous-violet, crimson-refining confessions
Of the Parthenon-twilight sun,
A renaissance of the diastolic-crystalline self
Into the first saffron-petaled intuitions and purple-sceptered
   breaths of the evening wind.

THE SOUL OF THE FOREST

When you walk between the two amber-majestic,
Dusk-ethereal pines at the Artemis-wreathed edge
Of the amaranth-celestial forest and tread softly,
Mellifluously on the golden-brown needles
Your soul enters forever the pristine-evolving domain
Of vernal-flaming vigils and you become forever
A part of the soul of the Ruisdael-burgeoning forest

Within the Thoth-sacred grove
A red and a white candle
On the primrose-permeating sides of a Chartres-
Breathing amaryllis-spire on a Tintern-fusing
Spectrum of silently receding mahogany-glass

Where the moon plays a cypress-vined fiddle
Of mellifluous-mazed light as the sun shapes
Emerald-scented pilasters of Nostell-leavening
Timelessness

Where yellow-teeming melodies of renascence-veined
Light perceive pink-rustling assonances of anemone-
Diastolic, apocalyptic-magenta dawn.

MOTHER NATURE

On a lily-bathing star of moist-apocryphal light
She waits for crescent-almandine echoes of iris-
Madrigal suns

In a silent corner of Stonehenge-auburn fields
She waits for phoenix-sceptered footsteps of grail-
Billowing exodus shaping the wind in pristine-
Marigold asters of delta-germinating, peacock-
Diapason truths

Along the zodiac-lavender horizon
She waits on a saffron-gloaming butterfly-dream
of amaryllis-jade, damask-palladium light

In lotus-streaming, crystalline-sage omens
Of jasmine-fermenting, Cawdor-astered radiances
She weaves carmine-crescent spells and isabella-soft
Smiles of porcelain-calyx swans on magenta-
Architraved haloes of oasis-cairned, sapphire-
Prismed timelessness.

The Light of the Dance

The morning trees dance pearl-cusped ballets
Of albemarle-moist, jasmine-floating light
Along juniper-gusting preludes of mauve-electric
Dusks the morning trees perceive the heart
Of the dawn in a cypress-lintelled pool of lavender-
Raising light healing the wounds of labyrinthine-
Angled darkness in auburn-crystalline, polonaise-
Resonating harmonies of empyrean-solitary words
In Goldau-exalting convergences of Powis-arborealis-
    philomel-ripples

The morning trees carve the emerald-lyred, melisma-
    immaculate
Intimations of the day on the mazurka-vocative, marigold-
Chastening edge of the horizon in hierophant-crimson,
    Atlantis-
Engulfing vortices of Gemini-tentacled light
Heron-gnostic signs of pristine-orphic sanctuaries
Of timelessness foretelling the inevitable decline
Of calico-gesturing mortality in clover-weaving calyxes
Of luminescent-astered, alpine-mazed infinities
In Belvoir-effulgent synergies of andante-cascading,
Cerulean-congealing aureoles

Listen to the music of the light with the harp-singing,
Ambrosia-pulsing vision of your saffron-numinous inner
    soul
The light of the dance is the music of eternity.

OF PHOENIX-DEWED CONSTELLATIONS

A capriccio-pulsating pool of obelia-blossoming,
Terpsichore-poised light shaping the nightingale-
    confessing,
Angelus-weaving sky in dusk-emerald triptychs of muslin-
Terraced stone-echoes and Llanberis-sacred liminal-sighs
Of hyacinth-chastening, Venetian-lyred dreams conceiving
Its own silver-immaculate wisdom in the incarnate radiance
Of pink-leavening zephyrs enclosed in sea-revolving
    hieroglyphs
Of orchid-soaring, Everest-tendering light transforming
The dark-thorned ravages of time in phoenix-dewed
    constellations
Of clover-pinioned, eglantine-murmuring eyes redeeming
Legato-hermetic silences in pyramid-astered, Aeolian-
    autumnal tears.

LET THE SOUL OF NATURE BE YOUR SOUL

Let the vast-meadowed fragrance of amber-ethereal
Poppy-truths lull you to sleep in Elysian fields
Of phantasmal-pale cloud-silences, let the blue-seeking
Solitude absorb your soul in jade-sated infinity
Let the soul of Nature be your soul
Let it guide your life in concentric-evolving circles of
    saffron-diapason light
Let it enchant your soul in Arcadian-moist
    rhythms of violet-curving moor-spells
When the clock on the mantlepiece of God
    runs down it is only the artist who revives
    the flow of eternity in Pleiades-divine harmonies
        of pristine-gesturing, lunar-webbed light,

Let the soul of Nature fill your soul
With amorphous-sentient, mantra-soaring tremors
Of eternity with Petworth-incandescent revelations
    of tessera-red, Eden-templed clouds
Let the soul of Nature fill your soul
With Thoth-preserving radiances of marigold-liminal,
Emerald-pledging light with fiery-celestial adorations
Of earth-trancing, white-animating estuary-plumes
When the festival-clock in the eye
Of the divinity fails it is only the poet
Of autumn-perpetuating twilight who will save
The sunset-gloaming luminescence of eternity,

Let the soul of Nature be your soul
In azure-dewed, Abydos-deepening melodies
Of honeysuckle-glistening, Utenwarf-echoing light
Let the soul of Nature be your soul
In nightingale-profound dreams of pristine-carmine,
Myrtle-folding mirrors and Endymion-ringed reveries
Of calyx-conceiving, yellow-gyrating light
When the maenad-stone clock collapses
In the crimson-fulfilling waves it is only the artist,
The poet, the dancer who saves the world
In a litany-diffusing, rainbow-perfecting cascade
Uniting light and color in primordial-sage,
Nocturne-flaming harmonies transposing mortality
Into flawless reflections of the Harewood-saffron,
Cerulean-expanding vortex of infinity
Transcending time in acropolis-discoursing
Inner sunrises of inestimable longing
And allegro-spinning, platinum-soaring light.

THE ANEMONE-GREEN EYES OF EVENING

I watch the anemone-green eyes of evening
Convene stray filaments of auburn-burgeoning
Time in Kellie-golden oracles of willow-
Sapphire breezes along the purple-stamened
Edge of the lily-misting, poplar-molten lake,

Softly germinating waves in cosmic memories
Of ancient-lavender silences and cinnabar-vellum
Marsh-blooms creating Schleswig-jade helixes
Of acropolis-leavening, kithara-threshing light,

Angular-warm tremors of eternity rippling
Portinari-frail surfaces in crystal-engraving
Murmurs of algae-elusive obelisks, shaping
Ochre-glowing time in cathedral-acanthus nocturnes
Of amaryllis-palomar, Lucerne-hermetic wisdom.

The Home of the Butterflies

The home of the butterflies
Is an emerald-hyacinth pool of Promethean-
Boundless light encompassing red-flaming
Trees of willow-gentian eyes

The home of the butterflies
Is an alpine-pinnacled dance of spring
A wisteria-crying nostalgia for the silence
Of the infinite for the sound of alpha-
Interwoven, glass-dewed harmonies

The home of the butterflies
Is a nightingale-epiphanic constellation
Of crystalline-silver, marble-veined spaces
A simultaneity of sun and moon
Where pearl-arching empires of seraphic-
Liminal light congeal in amaranth-gloaming mirrors

The home of the butterflies
Is an astral-tendrilled reverie
Of Apollonian-onyx unities
An orange-jade-streaming veil
Of tympanum-sceptered, lily-altared light

A Castalian-veined intuition of anemone-
Widening light where the helicon-sentient
Clouds fold time in albemarle-soaring
Rivulets of daemon-eclectic, Nile-glazed
Timelessness where the soul becomes a lunar-
Webbed chrysanthemum of pyramid-expanding
Eternity

A Protean-autumnal silence of hermetic-
Dreaming, horizon-marrowed light where
The souls of twilight-amber valences
Convene the iris-germinating, jasmine-
Permeating hearts of the odyssey-saving
Universe.

A Maya-Purple Flower

The branch of a plum tree extends its minuet-compassing
    eyes
On chrysanthemum-dewed silences into the almond-
    blossoming
Heart of the silver-crepuscular sea of longevity

A maya-purple flower of dawn-vernal, violin-pleated light
Binding the sky with magenta-pastel murmurs
Of Luxembourg-spiring garland-cadenzas

A rondo-venerating tendril creating nightshade-
Humming horizons of Thames-spectral light
In staccato-embroidered dreams of yellow-
Impassioned melodic-resolutions

A lento-textured bloom of gladiolus-ethereal,
Lavender-suave light scattering time
In Danube-curving streams of larkspur-compassionate,
Muse-inflecting words

A sapphire-reflective veil of amaryllis-muraled light
Sealing time in delphinium-tendrilled frescoes
Of contrapuntal-pinioned arabesques shaping timelessness
In Apollonian-soaring, dusk-blooming hearts
Of dithyramb-illuminating, pine-gloaming silences.

THE DIVINATIONS OF THE WIND

Listen to the divinations of the wind in dusk-spiritual
Scherzos of Elgin-centrifugal light, let the wind fill
Your soul with diaphanous-white, heron-innocent stamen-
Odes of diadem-effervescent, Lanhydrock-glistening light,
The clouds are the madrigal-pristine, windmill-illuminating
Hearts of divine spirits evolving the earth, rising,
And wandering across Promethean-spanning, andante-
   widening
Horizons, searching for renaissance-mazed reflections
Of their eternal home
Let the wind shape your soul in calyx-gloaming wisps
Of emerald-germinating, Stourhead-rapturing light
Let the wind seep into the innermost depths of your spirit
Minuet-serene, syrinx-ethereal tremors of chrysalis-amber
Eternity as the night permeates the sky in millenial-astered
Incantations of marigold-diapason, Atlantis-pulsing
   shadows.

A New Jersey Sunset

On a road in the Elysian-trembling, Osiris-leavening
Epoch between Princeton and Barnegat Bay
I entered a Church-vaulting sunset of Euganean proportions
A twilight vision of endless-gelatinous, cenotaph-porous
Eternity in carmine-burgeoning, astral-miranda echoes
Of manna-orange, ancient-timbered horizons
For a prolonged timeless moment I was in the Delphic-
Sunset vortex rising on purple-wandering helixes
Of alabaster-counterpaned light on a solitary-ripening
     chord
Of pink-tempera horizon somewhere in the heart
Of a savannah-whorled tropical-universe gazing
At a towering Amazon-balalaika waterfall
In pristine syllables of orchid-lavender oracles

I breathed in the andante-lavender fragrance
Of an Hippocrene-dewed flower shaping my soul
In diastolic-amber peals of the blossom of eternity,
I saw the architectonic murmurs of hidden kelp-valleys
Of radiolarian light shaping sonar-furrowing satellites
Of island-clustering, tangerine-dryadic winds,
I heard the heart of God beating on onyx-soft tremors
Of cinnabar-jade leaves breathing diamond-gloaming
     capillaries
Of white-cypress light into kithara-apsed margins of
     eternity.

The Wind Is a Dionysian Sharing

The wind is a divine mind
Of featherless, motionless luminescence

The wind is a St. Anthony lament of the dead
A fragile-streaming solstice-prophesy of Siddhartha

The wind is a Dionysian sharing of time
In pristine voices of bronze-pressed asters
And saffron-sheltering, Botticelli-scented camellias

The wind is a transatlantic mirror of crocus-mazed light
A Primavera resonance of Aristotle
Contemplating the bust of Homer

The wind engraving indigo-vaulted paroxysms
Of Avalon-incandescent wisdom on crystal-
Auburn lithotints of time.

Two Monarchs

Two small monarchs in the threshold tonality
Of Wessex-streaming, apocalyptic-red strands
Of pearl-carving light among Bosch-stained rushes
And indigo-primeval canopies of slate-onyx time,
Two monarchs on the edge of an Egeskov-silent brook
Molding marble-orange petals of light in gentian-
Black furrows of poppy-consuming weir-reveries,
A monarch transforming Himalayan time
Into cypress-winnowing fibers of fluorescent-apsed moss
A monarch shaping Alsen time
Into saffron epitaphs of immortal-scented sunflowers,
Two fragile-diapason monarchs gracefully crossing
Into soft-cinnabar megaliths of ancient cathedral-
Voices and purple-enameled flames of eternity
And back again to the lily-spawning, marsh-vaulting
    horizon.

IN SWAN-GLOAMING BLOSSOMS

A delphinium-blue afternoon sky saturates
The onyx-silver horizon in lily-adagio
Phoenix-wings of Borghese silences and amaryllis-jade
Helixes of Vedic-quantum silences,
Amber-silicon cataract-pulses of cypress-wombed hours
Congeal in cedar-veiling, saffron-acacia suspensions
Of ethereal-gray, sphinx-scented clouds,
Aureole-ivory breaths of light suffuse the sky
In swan-gloaming blossoms of diamond-orange,
    temple-dewed light.

MIRANDA-GERMINATING VEILS

Mandrake-burgeoning, soft-angled lichens
Spreading Bruegel-conjuring whispers of ageless beauty
Over tawny-ochre, serpentine-emerald tones
Of the ancient glade absorbing the oriel-curving,
Amethyst-canticled light of the aurora-sophic,
Hyacinth-astered sun

Minerva-radiating silences of Adirondack-westerly winds
Making trees prophetic, shaping Cézanne-astral hands
In apparitional-dewed gestures of pristine-lavender
Delight pervading Phidias-vined gates of maroon-stamened
Glass-aureoles with jonquil-maned murmurs of amber-
Perfumed, jasmine-ethereal light

Miranda-germinating veils of Chopin-vaulting light
Mediating between time and eternity inventing ribbon-frail
Crystals of Danube-membraned algae in kaleidoscope-
    domed
Masks of pandora-amicable synergies gazing at the sea
In larkspur-delicate, anemone-lambent moments
Of Orangerie-mutual transformation.

THE MIMOSA-LAVENDER RIPPLES

The mimosa-lavender ripples of the pristine-
iridescent lake are the first amaranth-wise
tremors of eternity shaping breaths of evening
wind in crystalline-elusive, Corot-symphonic

Silences of saffron-gloaming butterflies sealing
dusks of timelessness in lilac-glistening arbors
of helicon-mazed willow-dreams

The amber-dewed, madrigal-sheaved clouds of Eroica-
luminescent evening are the first iris-pealing
solitudes of the divine apocalypse blossoming

In crimson-ethereal, Merevale-almandine synergies
of diaspora-veined, marigold-exalting light.

THE VOICES OF THE CLOUDS

In the Murnau-red wind the voices of the Chillon-reflecting
Clouds scatter minaret-azure dreams of sunset-diffuse graves
Across orange-tympanum horizons in amethyst-pealing,
Norham-solitary tears of laurel-veined, lemon-diastolic
    light

The cathedral-transmuting voices of the Fontainebleau-
    ascending
Nepheliads sing nightingale-inviolable epiphanies of
    ancient-
Crystalline vastness where fiery-pastel asphodels bloom
In the saffron-opulent eyes of the palomar-isled divine
In crimson-lambent cascades of Isis-lyred resonances

In the narcissi-tremulous wind I hear the Vestal-pale
    reveries
Of twilight-vaned cloud-poppies spanning cosmic-
    diaphanous
Inundations of amaryllis-cinnabar stars across Waddesdon-
    timeless
Voices of white-ripening, turquoise-deepening spaces.

IN THE TEMPEST-DRIVEN HEART

In the Glamis-pristine stillness of the jasmine-knolled,
Saffron-helicon glade I see the marble-columbine silences
Of the past waiting for emerald-astered galaxies
To nurture them to alpine-bowered fronds of hyacinth-
Conjuring delight

In the tempest-driven heart of the primrose-streaming
Pines I hear a melisma-wild shape rise to meet muse-
Weaving visions of the heliotrope-blossoming sky, amber-
Veined reveries of gazebo-solemn vows germinating
Lily-deepening pools of Wynyates-madrigal light

In the Paphos-tameless whirlwinds of the linden-pulsing,
Amethyst-purifying forest I see the solstice-revering souls
Of Minerva-ancient sycamores listening to Florentine-
    mazed
Amplitudes of dithyrambic-glistening, vermilion-angled
    light
Yearning for nocturne-gladiolus wings of sphinx-resolving,
Amaryllis-incandescent diasporas.

THE KINETIC-AUTUMN WIND

At the dyke-fluttering edge of the ark-poised horizon
The Windsor-gloaming aureole-vortex is the Virgo-
Refulgent gaze of the agape-burgeoning divine
In arborealis-pulsing, myrtle-congealing waves
Of aster-soaring light, Goldau-listening seagulls
Wandering in a tympanum-softening pastiche
Of delta-phosphorescent lulls miles from ocean
Havens, Archimedean-veiled swallows floating
Across juniper-duned, zodiac-cascading silences
Where the kinetic-autumn wind conceives solstice-
Magenta, hibiscus-shaping dreams of saffron-
Anemone, Atlantis-converging light.

THE SNOW-SHOWER

The snow-shower is a pearl-misting waterfall
Of mercurial-shadowed incense lost from magenta-arked
Chalices of emerald-androgynous light by divine
Memories dispersing cypress-pergola omnipresence
    across maroon-cusped thresholds

Corinthian-astered shapes of ancient-tabernacle silences
And gargantuan-mullioned silhouettes of Phidias-
Chancelled willow-cairns congealing time
In crystalline-jagged epitaphs of fate-tendrilled winds
    pulsing myrmidon-tallow reflections

Of white-enameled whispers into pitch-apertured,
Dusk-arable abysses of shale-rarefied breaths
And astral-orange light where solstice dimensions
Of perpetual-sage souls transform moist-calyxed
Filigrees of time into millenial-pealing
    redemptions of eternity.

THE MIST PEOPLE

In a tetrahedral-mazed river of grey-knelled
Fog the mist people rise to watch the sky
Vanish in a purple-cymbal haze of mandrake-
Androgynous winds

Towns and villages masked and moved by crocus-
Alabaster splashes of sulphurous-circled light
Into another dimension of time
Where the mist people reign on auburn-marble,

Nemi-apocalyptic thrones of delta-winged clouds
As the silver-layering sea washes time away
Into a Balleroy-frescoed lagoon of hibiscus-
Jettied, calypso-leavening dreams;

The mist people shaping a new blue flower
Of Delphic-gloaming, saffron-pealing light
In the leviathan-veined, mobile-swirling atrium
Of the philomel-sacred, mimosa-reflecting glade

When diamond-pulsing eyes of almandine-shelled
Light conceive archipelago-crimson veils
Of Wallington-evolving, narcissus-fragile dusks.

IN PRISTINE-EFFULGENT HEARTS

In the auburn-spectral light of the dawn
The adoration of angels conceives chrysanthemum-
Dewed soliloquies of primeval-gesturing light
As the evergreen-adamanthine breeze convenes
Voices from the beginning and the end of time
Shaping intimations of mural-fermata galaxies
In pristine-effulgent hearts of helicon-orange,
    asphodel-germinating melodies;

The astral-soft silences rise
In crystalline-turquoise, wisteria-luminescent
Auras as saffron-emerald epiphanies
Of Apollonian-sage light peal across amaranth-
Blossoming sarabandes of Scone-exalting light
Shaping the heliotrope-angled silences
Of the morning in amethyst-helixed incantations
Of orphic-weaving, sunflower-ringed
    synergies.

A Pythian-Sacred Epiphany

Among ancient-towering oaks and sunset-liminal pines
There is a golden-iridescent, Dunster-majestic castle
Where crimson-sated roses and orange-diapason tulips
Blossom in perpetual-evolving synergies of apricot-
Effulgent, jade-crystalline light where Aeolian-lyred
Souls cherish the autumnal beauty of saffron-lambent,
Iris-helixed eternity, a Pythian-sacred epiphany
Of solstice-souls shaping the horizon in astral-elusive
Convergences of Cassandra-lambent genesis in pink-
Almandine pulsations of asphodel-soaring chimes
As the Amstel-westering wind paints gladiolus-maned,
Calliope-veined dreams across the grail-latticed sky
In diastolic-gloaming amplitudes of honeysuckle-
Sibylline light.

THE FLOWER OF ETERNITY

A lavender-cloistered haven on a cypress-ardent island
In the middle of a palm-breathing, russet-trembling
Windermere-reverie where the damask-inventing,
    ultramarine-
Iridescent flower of eternity assimilates flames
Of verbena-resined bloom, an embryo of palatine-
    rhododendron,
Orange-spindling light dispersing lunar-rippling seeds
Of Janus-stamened life, promontory-apsed veins of
    diamond-
Mullioned timelessness concentrated in dusk-heaving hearts
Of candelabra-enamelled stones conscious of Fauve-
Immutable inner harmonies instinctively listening
To the dynastic-tendrilled wind shaping the voice of
    eternity
In jade-ringed reflections of rainbow-preserving, aureole-
Murmuring silences, stones only touched by rhapsodic,
Curving breaths of a few immortal souls watching over
The saffron-restoring, muse-resplendent sublime.

Of Auburn-Etching Lazarus

Ivy-trellised rhythms of saffron-furrowing light
Converge the divine-softening eye in cypress-fluent
Haloes of luminous-lavender topiary-lullabies
Brushing across amoebae-tinted capillaries of olive-
Sated time where a blue-marrowed wave of Aegean-
    almandine
Sunlight marvels at a yellow-spectral sage of manna-
Chastening light; sun-channeling covenant-tremblings
Of auburn-etching Lazarus console emerald-sulphurous
Rose-brocades of primula-astered time in autumnal-silver
Helixes of orchid-blossoming dreams
And dahlia-crystalline, Salisbury-arching
Rainbow-metamorphoses.

At the Heart of the Waterfall

At the pearl-streaming vortex of the ambrosia-tendrilled
Cascade is a marigold-pristine, Chopin-effulgent blossom
Of jasmine-apocalyptic eternity in a wisteria-trellised vase
Of cobalt-blue epiphanies and diamond-lintelled shadows
Shaping the magenta-softening silences of the morning
In Danube-spectral estuaries of unearthly delight carving
Amethyst-dewed soliloquies of dusk-healing cloud-halos
On the emerald-leavening, Daubigny-seminal dreams
Of the mandolin-sceptered wind singing the Venus-globed
Murmurings and Astarte-melisma confluences of lavender-
Madrigal light in chrysalis-vaned synergies of symphonic-
Amber blooms at the damask-prismed heart
Of the Renoir-lambent, anemone-glistening waterfall.

A Clock Rides Upon the Sea

A clock rides upon the sea in a sedan
   chair of astral-trembling light
A cloud seeds the sky in hermetic
   intimations of aquamarine violins
A mist of Aphrodite-silvering melancholy
   saves the amaryllis-plunging curves of the sunset
A thought of the divine congeals
   in an amphora of equinoctial light
A web of muse-whispering silences
   transforms time in mandolin-intuitive masks
   of crescent-apertured shadows
A piazza of synthetic-diagonal wafers
   pronounces the lunar-suspending order
   of the orphic-mazed harlequin
A line of diamond-margined music staffs
   agitates the sumptuousness of mortality
A détente of curvilinear-pink harpsichord-
   convergences and heart-vaulting tower-murals
   prophesies the purity of the blue-sacramental circle
A mountain of yellow-sailing light
   plays asphodel-pristine chords of perpetual-
   sage harmonies across cypress-layered dreams
     of Castalian springs.

IN THE MIST-LADEN SILENCES

In the mist-laden silences of the autumn-gentian aura
Of hydrangea-spectral timelessness the elves chant
Amber-trellised lullabies of the hibiscus-fluent sunset-
Apocalypse as the Manet-glistening vase congeals
In mimosa-tetrahedral exigencies of alabaster-
Cairned, cyclamen-fermenting, Cassandra-pulsing genesis
In the Venetian-purple, calliope-labyrinthine solitudes
Of the dahlia-luminescent grove of kaleidoscope-yellow,
Crystalline-jade peace the sapphire-astered hummingbirds
Sing silver-auguring metamorphoses of cobalt-lintelled,
Meissen-orange light as the evening wind whispers ruby-
Ancestral dreams of marigold-germinating butterflies
Into Renoir-vermilion, sibylline-ardent tapestries
Of Chambord-lambent, forsythia-breathing light.

THE FIRST SOUNDS OF SPRING

An aureole-mazed breath of light burgeoning softly
Suddenly among gray-torrential, sphinx-sceptered clouds,
A divine spark of onyx-white lucidity giving life,
Radiating iris-diastolic blossoms of fugal-trembling
Life across windmill-sharing memories and Breakers-
Luminescent reveries of evening horizons,
A camellia-marble breath of pure damask-prismed light
Pulsing the first moments of auburn-jonquil mandalas
In moist-jade tendrils of sea-fevered dreams,
Shaping the first sounds of spring in amber-gray willows
Of lunar-rippling, diamond-apocalyptic light and soft-
Languishing, cyclamen-solstice prayers of russet-
Spiring winds, floating Easter-stamened lilies
In amaryllis-empyrean estuaries of mandrake-germinating,
Arcadian-lavender sunrises.

A Madonna

A madonna among the soft-prismed apples slowly
Shaping rivulets of zinnia-exulting, acacia-
Consecrating timelessness along velvet-sirocco
Curtains of dream-furling, ivory-plumed light
As the saffron-gelatinous wind breathes dahlia-
Fetal shadows across Ephesian-gloaming hills of
Red-onyx palms, a face of obelisk-radiant depths
And evening-fermenting silences sealing Katmandu-
Lavender timelessness in crocus-culminating aureoles
Of Maya-lemon hibiscus-doves.

OF SACRED-ANEMONE SILENCES

When the sea washes upon the shore
In the late afternoon it leaves traces
Of divine silences and saffron-exulting
Truths, traces of ancient religions and
Distant mythologies which the children
Pick up and cast away as broken,
Extraneous seashells on delta-wandering
Filigrees of Poseidon-whispering spray

When the sea floats upon the evening shore
Marble-auguring omens of other galaxies
And Gemini-soft pallors of eternity
The children think they look pretty
As pink-silken ribbons blowing carelessly,
    loosely in the breeze

When the sea washes its carmine-soaked
Tears upon the twilight shore the children
Laugh and play catch and try to capture
A fiddler crab nestled in the sand

When the sea washes its last swells
Of sunset-stained star-embryos upon
The candle-knelled shore only broken-
Prismed traces of sacred-anemone silences
And Atlantis-permeating aureoles linger
At the crimson-luminous, sulphurous-circled
Edge of eternity.

ALONG THE AVALON-MISTING SHORE

Elysian-petaled seashells strewn along the Avalon-
Misting shore in moor-globed tides of laser-blue,
Alzinen-spinning thoughts, emerald-mimosa
Annunciations of Poseidon-radiant sunlight
Glistening along crimson-drenched thresholds
Of algae-languishing, soft-barnacled time,

Andromeda-amber silences floating crepe-myrtle
Mantra-swallows of pandora-philomel light
Across St. Petersburg-resonant incantations
Of russet-orange dominions and maroon-havened
Prophesies of Vermeer-softened lucidity,

Auburn-concentric pulsations of Elbe-tinted sunsets
Streaming cerebral-jade poppies of calliope-
Aquamarine silences into cypress-expansive caverns
Of metropolitan-mercurial time.

BRONZE-PARABLED LEAVES

Ahimsa-stamened time drips from ginger-evolving
Leaves like almond-scented honey from autumn-
Sheaved, Nirvana-moist combs
Locust-molten blooms of Ghent-oleander light
Shaping the edge of time from sepia-chaliced
Tremors of the Tibetan-fugal evening wind
Bronze-parabled leaves searching for peregrine-
Jade souls, waiting to congeal as acacia-golden
Butterflies in the patient hands of the palomar-divine
Pale-willowed wings flying south in an orange-
Templed glaze of Shiva-pulsating mists
Gemini-aureole leaves spilling time into chalices
Of yellow-terracotta light, shaping eternity
In ancient-emerald mirrors of platinum-sheer obelisks.

THE PURIFICATION

Let the platinum-quivering waves ripple through
Your hands in crocus-ethereal surges of sunset-
Globed silences, let the carmine-maenad chimes
Of the snow-porcelain sea flow through the salmon-
Duned ventricles of your soul in miranda-languishing
Echoes of limestone-burgeoning time at the Euterpe-
Lavender threshold of life, let the silver-moist light
Of the sea cleanse your mind in soft-diaphanous
Tonalities of Venetian-white nocturnes, let the ocean
Feel your abalone-enchanted love for the saffron-eternal
Truth of its mimosa-scarlet, magi-discoursing horizon.

LET THE AUTUMN FILL YOUR SOUL

Let the autumn fill your soul with Elysian-cosmic
Sadness with the hydrangea-fluted melancholy
Of piazza-apparitional evanescence as impetuous, red
Leaves glisten through your hands for only the soul
Embalmed in Dogana-wise sadness can prophesy
His own imminent, unvanquished eternity
In Zoroastrian silences of magenta-crystalline light
Let the sea fill your crocus-raptured soul
With astral-mazed chasms of sapphire-tameless,
Giorgione-melodious light
The Belton-twilight wind shapes the darkness
In odyssey-silver chimes of daemon-ethereal loveliness
As the sea seals time in Florentine-pale eyes
Of lapis lazuli-wandering sculptures of amber-
Vaulting, hyacinth-echoing light.

OF HELIOTROPE-MIMOSA DAWN

I walk out of marble-dewed, willow-meticulous silences
Of the evening-crenellated abbey into crocus-
Sceptered lights of pink-chrysanthemum suns
And Iris-astered, dusk-unvanquished resonances
Of amethyst-effulgent Indian-summers
As Hyperion weaves Lorelei-softening traces
Of gypsy-dreaming time into polymer-stamened
Haloes of auburn-telestar castles
As Sappho scatters plum-crested waves
Of alabaster-edged memories into Hibernian-
Coved epiphanies of kithara-beige light
I walk among the sepulchral-latticed breaths
Of bronze-whispering light listening
To the crimson-sage swallows whispering
Alluvial-ochred spells of heliotrope-mimosa,
    orange-acanthus dawn.

In Mimosa-Yellow Incantations

As the mist clears I see apocalyptic-white angels
    playing the Chillon-auguring ritual of timelessness
    in Dogana-yellow globes of lily-breathing,
        astral-latticed light

As the mist clears I see twilight-amber
    temple-pallors falling upon the castle ruins
    engraved in myrrh-evening, azalea-diaphanous
        silences

As the mist clears I see the hyacinth-golden light
    emanating from the eye of the divine shaping
    sacred-alluvial tremors of eternity reunifying
        amethyst-sealing wisdoms of ancient-textured
        horizons with cypress-wandering islands

Of Jungfrau-pristine gladiolus-truths, when the mist
    clears I see marigold-seraphic butterflies dissolving
    time in mimosa-lavender incantations of diamond-
    ethereal, autumn-helixed light.

THE TREE OF LIFE

The morning tree is the congealed silence
Of the divine shaping the aura of eternity
In Elysian-green inflections of amaryllis-
  pristine light
The afternoon tree is a ring-vaulting dusk
Of mandrake-dewed elixirs conceiving sapphire-
Weaving chalices of Crathes-gloaming light
The evening tree is a damask-prismed veil
Of albemarle-deepening, Athena-sacred truths
Forming the horizon in astral-mazed amplitudes
Of Burghley-effulgent reveries
The night tree is an Aeolian-crystalline cathedral
Of asphodel-soaring nocturnes enshrining
The turquoise-misting, hibiscus-pleated sea
In elven-sacred, golden-chrysalis voices
Of ancient-prophetic, auburn-pealing
  forest-dawns.

THE SUNSET CLOUDS

The sunset clouds are almandine-soft, chamomile-
Straying angels of palomar-isled, Newport-eaved light
Magenta-pealing mournings of serpentine-angled,
Levitan-astered light amaryllis-pulsing, Dogana-
Sentient echoes of tiffany-acanthus, lotus-harped light
Shaping the Amazon-undulating, Elbe-celebrating
Cornucopia of anemone-burgeoning, iris-glistening life
In dynastic-sapphire, lemon-crystalline rings
Of lilac-germinating, tangerine-helixed melodies
Suspending time long enough for primordial-cinnabar
Castalian-souls to enter the Maggiore-veined,
Uffizi-valed prism of bronze-gloaming,
Gladiolus-rapturing eternity.

OF GLYNDE-SPACIOUS ETERNITY

I listen to the dusk-pealing amaryllis-lambent silences
Of ancient-lacquered shadows meandering
Through jade-apsed clearings of Camelot-enthroned
Wilderness as the hourglass-congealing breeze
Radiates violet-weaving whispers in heliotrope-
Softened crannies of agaric-widening tombs

I am the white-cairned, lotus-astered perpetuity
Of stone-martyred silences suspending gray-stained
Dooms of Venus-thorned light in lavender-oracular
Cupolas of Delphic-crystalline, Eroica-unvanquished
Reveries;

I feel the cypress-consoling silences of the Barlach-
Reciting stones in my hands lichen-dreaming etudes
Growing into my hands nepenthe-pallid euphonies
Filling my hands with andante-coronal pulsations
Of onyx-inner, alcaic-saving wisdom

I feel the Rodin-elegiac stones sharing pantheon-
Moist whispers of Glynde-spacious eternity
With auburn-resined bands of mourning-dappled
Flesh shaping my hands in dusk-glistening
Intimations of crescent-apertured, gold-enflaming
Light.

OF GOLDEN-MELTING HEARTS

An amaranth-gloaming field enclosed by marble-dewed,
Thistle-lucid polygons of acanthus-timeless, red-alabaster
Poppies and sapphire-gladiolus, dusk-crystalline silences
A madrigal-yellow, lily-burgeoning reverie of seraphic-
Luminescent, Euterpe-crescent tendrils of eternity
And Turin-vernal pirouettes of Atlantis-mazed, amaryllis-
Prophetic light folding time into spiral-glowing, amethyst-
Horizoned ravines of apocalypse-scented salmon-ice
Beyond Ganges-streaming, Castalian-rhythmed resonances
Of immortal wisdom pealing time from millennial-lambent,
Maroon-stamened mountains of albatross-immaculate,
Tulip-perpetuating light shaping time into phoenix-moist,
Wisteria-breathing soliloquies of Elysian-whispering
Mirrors, a sycamore-opulent, chrysanthemum-confessing
    meadow
Revealing the Blenheim-amber, cypress-winding soul
Of the universe in pristine-effulgent, Artemisian-magenta
Nebulae of golden-melting, Aeolian-autumnal hearts.

THE AEOLIAN-SAGE WIND

I am a pink-arching, Stowe-iridescent effusion of cherry-
  white,
Orange-tendrilled blossoms suffusing amorphous-gray
  shadows
In silver-almandine whispers of chamomile-soaring
  harmonies
I am a twilight-eaved manor-aureole of sapphire-weaving
Ascensions shaping asphodel-lyred clouds in jade-
  cultivating,
Tiffany-leavening soliloquies
I am the Delphic-mazed longing of saffron-gloaming,
Pergola-animating silences sealing Stockholm-gentian
Cascades in auburn-gleaming reflections of emerald-
Pealing, iris-helixed eternity
I am the Aeolian-sage wind of the Virgo-refulgent evening
Sharing Seine-misting echoes of Easter-dewed light
With Sistine-pellucid reveries of Corot-lavender horizons
I am the seraphic-liminal synergy of amaryllis-cadenced,
Azalea-germinating dawns shaping the cypress-astered,
Bronze-chastening rainbow in crimson-diapason echoes
Of Paxton-effulgent, lilac-ambrosial dreams.

The First Autumnal Silences

Soft-white butterflies spin
The first autumnal silences
Over the incandescent-breathing leaves
Shaping yellow-congealing webs
Of bamboo-pleated light on stamen-lavender
Resurrections of prismatic-willow souls,
Marigold-virginal, labyrinthine-intuitive leaves
Emerging at the pink angel-conjuring heart
Of the kithara-sublime, lotus-altared tree
Two albatrosses of pearl-manging light
Soaring into the oasis-embalming horizon
Of jasmine-acropolis, alabaster-laminated light,
When the wind rustles the genesis-warm leaves
In metaphysical-jade reflections of divine-nomadic
Silences and ancient-liminal prayers of zodiac-
Germinating light I hear paradise-architraved
Calligraphies of amber-helixed, Orpheus-pulsing
Wisdom.

Autumn

Autumn is a delicate symphony
Of soft-madrigal swallows and albumen-
Crimson nirvanas of jen-amber light

Autumn is a diastolic epiphany
Of amaryllis-chancelled space, a systolic
Mirror of gelatinous-emerald time

Autumn is the cyclically reciprocal
Revelation of Nature and God
In a fragile symbiosis of seraphic-
Ascending visions and indigo-angled prisms
Of fern-camellia hieroglyphs

Autumn is the gathering of yellow-marrowed,
Cinnabar-jade ambrosia by a Buddha-wandering figure
For the iris-glowing soliloquies and silver-
Polygonal folds of her poppy-arching winter-dreams

Autumn is a crystal-dewed transformation of time
Into embryonic, dynastic-sharing trinities
Of honeycomb-diaphanous, magi-eternal light

Autumn is an inner radiance of vale-horizoned,
Saffron-conceiving leaf-souls of cypress-marble purity
Shaping new dimensions of acropolis-shadowed,
Helicon-pinioned timelessness.

THE SPACIOUSNESS OF THE RUISDAEL-LAMBENT CLOUDS

I am the spaciousness of the Ruisdael-lambent clouds
Spilling saffron-helixed amulets of asphodel-pure light
Into cerulean-sceptered, Goldau-pulsing dominions
I am the lily-architraved aura of onyx-ethereal,
Amstel-crystalline melodies of Artemisian-lavender
Timelessness shaping sphinx-pilastered reveries
Into hyacinth-lambent, Tintern-mimosa blooms
Of marble-veined, sapphire-pealing light
I am the Highclere-mazed serenity of the primrose-
Leavening, gladiolus-soaring horizon where pearl-misting
Circles of dahlia-pink, Eden-liminal hieroglyphs
Converge ruby-lacquered elegies of Luxor-dreaming spaces
And chrysalis-vermilion augurs of Florentine-gloaming
Dawns in emerald-chastening, lotus-weaving absolutions
Of astral-breathing, wisteria-shrining light.

WHERE THE DOVES GATHER

In the turquoise-blossoming, hieratic-red space
Of minaret-swathed olive trees is a Pergamon-
Centered grove of sunset-verdant, Caserta-eaved
Light where the willow-auguring doves gather
Every evening to weave the Murnau-consummate passing
Of the day in jonquil-crystalline, Giverny-streaming grails
Of amaryllis-dewed, acanthus-golden light in palomar-
Christening, cherry-trancing soliloquies of Isis-
Leavening, philomel-breathing light
An Aeolian-sanctified glade where the sapphire-pealing
Doves summon the Apollonian-sage spirits of poppy-
Consecrating, nirvana-vaned ancestors in magenta-
    diapason
Effusions of orphic-inner enlightenment where the Titian-
Graceful doves carve saffron-glistening rivulets
Of fugal-enchanted timelessness on Fauve-astered blooms
Of acacia-numinous, amaranth-gloaming light.

A Damask-Scrolled Fugue

The evening is a damask-scrolled fugue of amber-
Terracotta light shaped by solstice souls in hermetic-
Stringing, Himalayan-magenta dissolutions of time
And sacred-liminal harmonies of amaryllis-eaved helicon-
    solitudes
Solstice souls rising from sphinx-willowed,
Wessex-stamened silences creating Aeolian-lavender,
Brahman-pealing triptychs of twilight sky in dahlia-
Fermenting, cypress-exulting helixes of grail-sceptered,
Magnolia-tiffany reveries
Solstice souls carving mandolin-crimson intimations
Of Mahakala-lotus eternity on porcelain-gray cloud-
Monoliths of Rhine-primordial, juniper-breathing
Energy as the adagio-spectral wind perpetuates
Horus-anemone exodus in apocalyptic-christened,
Kithara-apsed amplitudes and autumn-lacquered, silver-
Leaf aureoles of Turner-iridescent, golden-architraved light.

A PYTHIAN-WISE LAKE

There is a Minerva-sacred lake
In the midst of the forest shaping the amber-
Lintelled reveries of the sunset in butterfly-
Mimosa apparitions of astral-symphonic light

An asphodel-breathing pool where chrysanthemum-
Embalming horizons fold into jade-tendrilled thresholds
Of orange-kithara diasporas where chrysalis-red wings
Of cypress-foaming vases convene turquoise-liminal
Voices of gardenia-pealing masks

An Orpheus-mazed stream where acanthus-glistening trees
Blossom rainbow-sentient clouds of auburn-pilastered
Light in the alpine-hallowed aura of marble-veined mists
Where Arcadian-lavender silences gather in cathedral-
Stamened rings of crepuscular-silver eyes

There is a Pythian-wise lake of nocturne-lambent
Solitudes sealing the heron-magenta, willow-vaned
Aura of timelessness in diamond-pulsing effusions
Of crystalline-almandine, lapis lazuli-conceiving light.

THE TWILIGHT-APOCALYPTIC REVERIE

The twilight-apocalyptic reverie is the purest
Crystalline-chancelled light of the evening sun
Amber-epiphanic annunciations of golden-veined,
Delphic-sated light suspend time in marble-
Perpetual haloes of Sesshu-solstice spirits
Wandering across sequoia-peristyled, cypress-vaulting
Thresholds, cobalt-glowing, cinnabar-rising
Effusions of orange-evolving, Parthenon-helixed light
Healing the wounds of mortality in saffron-gloaming
Ecstasies of translucent-magenta rainbows
Transforming Gautama-musing souls into Aeolian-damask,
Lily-diapason breaths of Vanderbilt-architraved,
Woburn-pristine light
Shaping the Easter-dewed hieroglyph of the horizon-
Leavening sun in amaranth-lavender memories
Of eternity as iris-stamened prophesies
Of porcelain-acanthus, maroon-prismed light
Open forever the bronze-pealing gates of paradise.

OF DIVINE-GLOAMING WISDOM AND EDEN-EXALTING SPACES

The Wings of Swans

In the wind I hear the gray-astered, fugal-converging
  silences
Of the divine floating against silicon-curving pillars
Of eternity swirling around agate-misting pilasters
Of ancient-templed shores, in the late-afternoon wind
I hear soft-alabaster voices speaking of millennial-white,
Contiguous dimensions of time where mortality is only
A prelude to reincarnation,
In the wind I hear empyrean-softened, ethereal-groved
  voices,
Blue-adamanthine reflections of juniper-cresting voices
Calling from cerulean-swathed mountain-amulets,
The late-afternoon wind breathes anemone-gelatinous
Omniscience through magenta-emerald gates
Of Brahman-pealing paradise,
In the wind I hear the wings of swans bearing souls
To Nirvana-rising thresholds of saffron-onyx light
In Atlantis-duned silences I hear fragile-violet
Kelp-winds from the Mycenaean wilderness beneath the
  waves
And astral-yellow cypress-winds from the end of the world
Shaping the immanent timelessness of the damask-weaving,
Nocturne-spinning self.

The Source of Immortal Time

Wandering through Oslo-blue flowers of chrysalis-
Golden dreams I see the embryo of immortal time
Pulsing vermilion-porcelain veils of dahlia-tensile
Light across the sable-altared edge
Of the acropolis-sunset sea

A magnetic-jade shaft of crimson-arborealis
Angles in an adagio-azure, madrigal-laminating
Pool of salmon-androgynous, camellia-eaved dawns
Radiating lichen-solstice dusks in lapis lazuli-
Expanding, Passacaglia-breathing mirrors of amaranth-
Crystalline, Elysian-converging light

Wandering through maroon-sceptered tulips
Of palladium-glistening, myrtle-calyx fields
I see the onyx-veiled source of immortal time—
A helicon-orange bouquet of magenta-translucent,
Amaryllis-leavening silences and marigold-
Chastening, Amstel-spacious light-murmurs—
In an Atlantis-crescent radiance of sylvan-
Parabled waterfalls and Sargasso-blossoming winds.

ECHOES OF ETERNITY

Along the hieratic-willow, moss-satyred pier
I see limestone-moist echoes of eternity
Floating across ancient-lintelled, Artemis-jade horizons
In mantra-rustling elegies of lily-trembling breezes,
In the pumice-architraved vortex
Of dactyl-inventing, crystal-eclipsing waves
I see the amber-prismed radiance
Of marble-Parnassus chimes scattering
Delphic-veined rivulets of dithyrambic time
Across marigold-embering sands of lunar-sheathed light,
Along the edge of asphodel-symphonic silences
I hear seagull-crimson, azure-perfecting murmurs
Of the Pythian-white clouds of eternity.

A SCULPTURE OF ORANGE-CHASMED LEAVES

A sculpture of orange-chasmed, Eucharist-eloquent leaves
And soft-marlin, columbine-triadic infinity rises
Through acanthus-vaulting traces of crescent-morning
    mists,
A white-veiled sculpture of ancient-lambent
Truth and tympanum-fugal silences scatters
Wild-anemone murmurs of Picasso-kithara light
Across Sistine-auguring fields and Flemish-ringed pools
Of lichen-glazed, cathedral-shaping solitudes,
The light of the marble-expanding sculpture
Infusing the light of the sun
With onyx-maroon pulses of divine-alcaic radiance,
The light of the silver-scrolled sculpture
Dissolving time in a Doric-floating mirror
Of crystalline-cypress, sublime-amber light.

THRESHOLD MOMENTS

It is only at threshold moments
That we are truly alive to the genesis-
Lavender beauty of the crystalline-
Architraved wind and to the divinity
Of the saffron-helixed light of our souls,

It is only at threshold moments
That we breathe Nirvana-almandine omens
Of alcaic-tessera light and transform
Our souls into perpetual-amber twilight-
Cadences of Sylt-vestal, wind-dreaming eternity;

The poem is a luminous-solstice epiphany
Of the transcendent and transforming self
In Apollonian synergies of Monet-burgeoning light
At the lemon-exulting, Lhasa-rippling threshold
Of eternity,

The poem is a Michelangelo-gloaming purification
Of ephemeral time, a transformation of mortality
In sacred-liminal, timeless-golden silences
Where the lyrically resonant spirit never changes
And the karma-soft, reincarnating soul never dies
The poem is a Limoges-pristine resurrection of the dusk-
Ripening self in purple-oracular, diamond-lintelled
Pools of eternity.

Four Sacred Forms

A castle of magenta-dewed, peacock-creched silences
And adamanthine-shearing, Parsifal-ranging soliloquies
Transforming vicissitudes of time
Into orange-cascading, pearl-fluting megaliths
Of Arnhem-resined, amphibrach-soaring light;

A castle of poinsettia-germinating, bronze-sublime
Harmonies of apocalyptic-crimson winds
Redeems white-shadowed caravans and jade-apsed crevices
Of spectral-vanishing carbuncle-energy in Vestal-
Sacred prophesies of Atman-thalassic, silver-equinoctial
    light;

A castle beyond scythe-laminated dreams of time
Beyond sable-totemic murmurings of mortality
A perpetual-amber eclipse of time in a majestic-
Martyred, magi-pristine cove of the Thames,
The Rhine, the Hudson, and the Ganges
A crystalline-leavened simultaneity of eternity
In poppy-wandering, dusk-sated thresholds
    of cypress-helixed light.

A Dahlia-Globed Oasis

A dahlia-globed oasis of saffron-mandarin light
Along a Corinthian-ethereal cove
Of the angel-pulsing, paladin-dusted river
A velvet-golden palace of a hundred majestic-
Amber spires of cinnabar-obelia light
Shaping jasmine-silken whirlpools of lavender-
Sated sky into Isis-cascading hieroglyphs
Of fern-winged light, agate-kithara tears
Of afternoon-delta winds transforming time-
Furling waves into onyx-pale reveries of Delphic
Oracles and Hampton-auburn helixes of pomegranate-
Lily hibiscus-dreams,
A palace of a thousand crimson-molten, lambent-
Orange crystal-windows holding the soft-pink light
Of eternity in anemone-spinning, damask-aureole
Mirrors, acropolis-spanning, purple-amethyst
Eclogues of Pindar-silver light conceiving
Windsor-architraved, grail-sceptered radiances
Of gladiolus-tendrilled, dusk-tympanum timelessness
In astral-delphinium, myrrh-gleaming arbors
Of frankincense-magenta, ambrosia-weaving haloes.

OF DUSK-GLOAMING MIRRORS

The Minerva-gentian light is the Elysian-pale radiance
Within the lotus-germinating soul beyond meridian-
External suns of myriad galaxies as intrinsically
Powerful as the Saltram-exalting light of the auburn-
Breathing chandelier illuminating the heliotrope-sheaved
Heart of Delphic-golden reflections only in a marble-
Pilastered, lily-converging vortex of dusk-gloaming mirrors
Is the light onyx-pure and Apollonian-soft only in a
    spacious-
Crenellated epiphany of sphinx-magenta auras and ogival-
    diapason
Chimes does the saffron-leavening light heal the wounds
Of mortality in lavender-asphodel, Harlaxton-winding
    silences.

140

AN ETHEREAL-SAGE CASTLE

An ethereal-sage castle appears near the Orangerie-
Enclosed lake when the amber-helixed, Theocritean-
Softening twilight pours across its Belvedere-cascading
Walls and disappears in the azalea-fountained light
Of the lapis lazuli tears of divine spirits dreaming
Of Palladian bridges I saw it once in my youth
When the Sistine-cairned elms reached Parham-giant
Shadows along the edge of the azure-swelling waters
When onyx-stained breezes whispered eglantine-streaming
Harmonies in maze-fermenting lullabies when madrigal-
    purple
Butterflies played upon saffron-gloaming rhythms
Of Zoroastrian-seminal light there is a Drumlanrig-liminal,
Moss-reflecting castle dividing transience from the
    asphodel-
Veined shadows of immortality sheltering the lemon-
    scrolled,
Dusk-lambent auras of eternity from ephemeral-gilded,
Sable-ewered exodus in the presence of the diamond-paned,
Opalescent-globed castle the questing soul reshapes itself
In dawn-perfecting calligraphies of phoenix-soaring,
Tyntesfield-effusive, emerald-calyxed light.

OF DIVINE-GLOAMING WISDOM

There is a savannah-lambent day when
The red-solstice pulse of eternity
Chastens lavender-entombed tears and mortal-
Laminating thoughts along Eurydice-marble
Matrices of odyssey-satyred winds
When the inner glow of saffron-Elysian light
Heals all the animate and inanimate life
And makes all things papyrus-whole, Maya-vaulting
Visions of divine-gloaming wisdom
When the sea and sky are an Apollonian-onyx
Unity of blue-albumen, gray-webbed light
A vermilion-profound reverie of oasis-
Alveolar intuitions encompassing amaryllis-pink,
Thrush-gracing cloud-helixes
Communing with Orpheus-noble beings
From a jasmine-remote, Lindau-binding curve
Of the yellow-polygonal horizon
A dynastic-anemone meiosis of Nepenthe-hyaline,
Zodiac-consecrating memory transforming pisces-sunset,
Morven-pendulous megaliths to hermetic-lavender
Murmurs of dove-winding eternity.

A TIMELESS MOMENT

A timeless moment when you see
The beginning and the end of time
When you see endless orchid-augurs
And eternal-spindling filaments of space
When you understand sapphire-swelling murmurs
Of the asphodel-lyred evening wind
When crocus-glistening, emerald-conceiving leaves
Of the soft-gnarled sycamore blow in Ruisdael-
   embering breezes
When you understand light-flowing rhythms
Of damask-rolling robin-speech,

A timeless moment when Sanskrit prophesies
Transforming passionate-palomar thresholds
Transmuting marigold-striated harp-whispers
Shape Dionysian helixes into ambrosial-lambent
Echoes of Apollonian-magenta infinities,

A timeless moment when the last rays
Of the sun possess all the wisdom of the world,
When all mortal wisdom
Is framed by a canticle of light
When all mortal wisdom
Rests on the mist-tapered ends of a great white pine
Alone in a corner of the amaryllis-inviolate,
Dusk-astered forest.

A Stone-Breathing Manor House

There is a stone-breathing manor house at the edge
Of town on a cypress-helixed meadow leading
To the Ionic-phosphorous center of the earth
Dark-crimson tunnels pulsating inner rhythms
Of diamond-mantled light across juniper-
Marrowed thresholds of coral-sheaved eternities
A hieroglyph-vaulting Shangri-La
On lily-rolling hills of soft-forgotten time
Majestic gardens of orchid-hibiscus dreams
Beyond sable-thrusting vicissitudes of transience
A soul-shaping Shangri-La of divine-fugitive silences
And amber-veined epiphanies of jasmine-amaryllis light
A Florentine-chancelled prelude of harp-musing truths
Inevitably flowing to other worlds of dusk-frescoed
Trinities and orange-prophetic, Turner-iridescent
   immortality
A marble-grottoed paradise of magi-murmuring winds
And maroon-syncopated sunset-vigils.

THROUGH MARBLE-MISTING EONS

A room where the saffron-helixed light of eternity
Fuses with the cypress-amber light of immortality
In a perpetual-sage, lotus-harped suspension of time,
A palomar-frescoed dimension of the timeless self
Sealed in dusk-crystalline tremors of Delphic-sated grace
And astral-dewed configurations of green-purifying infinity,
A Rembrandt-veined solstice soul safe forever from
The calico-jettied gestures and pitch-draped dreams
Of mortality pressed helplessly against adamanthine-
Veined, diamond-apteryx walls,
A solstice soul losing itself in maroon-prismed
    reincarnations
Of chrysalis-anemone voices radiating lavender-onyx
    cathedral-
Silences through moss-crenellated centuries and
    Appassionata-
Swelling, marble-misting eons of time.

The Figures in the Paintings

There is a time of day
When all the figures in the paintings
Emerge in the spaciousness of the room
When they sit on the divan or along
The mahogany table and talk freely
As if nothing had happened
As if their willow-murmuring essences
Were as perpetual as the cyclicality of nature
When they appear from gilded frames
And chiaroscuro eternities, from Gothic-liminal
Reveries and azure-unvanquished spaces
They never change endowed by the arabesque-golden,
Acanthus-lintelled enclosure with the Blickling-
Luminescent aura of marble-germinating eternity
They never fear the vicissitudes which ravage
The flux of the world and time
Shaping the tremors of the sea along the calyx-
Mazed dream of the horizon conceiving dune-scented
Meadows in diastolic epiphanies of yellow-exalting
Light in the ethereal-primrose, amphora-echoing
Gleam of Meissen-amber silences the figures fulfill
A twilight paradise in mandrake-eloquent shadows
Where lavender-resplendent asphodels and Delphic-
Pealing, lily-gloaming reveries never fade.

THE ANNUNCIATION

An angel of chrysalis-amber light consecrates
Cypress-haloed silences of eternity
In the presence of ethereal-fugal wisdom
Before the luminous-pulsing, Chartres-discovering dawn
The sunflower-lambent mother of the savior
Watching moist-adamanthine streams of saffron-vaulting
Light spill over a perpetual-rippling arbor
Of porcelain-white lilies and willow-inviolate,
Primrose-burgeoning horizons
An angel shaping crimson-scrolled eternity
In iris-domed, amethyst-stamened winds of marigold-
Diapason light swirling gently in warm-oleander,
Crystalline-sage epiphanies of dusk-timeless,
Amaryllis-incandescent grace.

OF ATLANTIS-SHAPING SOULS

In the monumental shadow of the White Mountains
There is an Eden-conscious, helicon-serene valley
Of lily-gloaming solitudes and onyx-lavender snowdrops
Where centuries ago a divine figure wandering
Across celestial domes of pale-acropolis dawns
Inadvertently dropped a vial of alabaster-fugal silences,
An Aeolian-charted vale of hawthorne-trellised
Timelessness where Atlantis-shaping souls live forever
In the emerald-lyred, Minerva-gentian beauty of nature
And in centripetal synergies of cypress-regenerating
Radiances, a crystal-vapored, ochre-sensitive valley
Of ethereal-marigold, pink-tessera light
Where time is a ravine-furrowed memory
Of Giza-shattered vows, a soft-forgotten echo
Of Parthenon-sated augurs,
A valley where the light of inner beauty
Is as infinite as the light of the sun.

THE PRISTINE TAPESTRY

Meissen vases shaped in silken-ochre
Pools of ancient-anemone pagodas,
Porcelain-lambent calyx-trinities lingering
On fragile-carillons Ming-thresholds
Of twilight-crocus moors, emerald-
Floating chalices of Luxor-pale light
Lost in sunken synergies of sand-corniced,
Rainbow-delta incantations,
Dynastic-frescoed pyramid-dews spread dawn-
Crystalline passions of amber-prophetic sunsets
And rosary-seething, toccata-membraned cantos
Across evergreen-pealing omens of Cytherean-
Syncopated centuries, immortal-filigree
Silences scattering the chiliastic-sceptered
Darkness in Hermitage-astered vigils
Of lilac-knotted, amaryllis-reflecting eternity.

SHAPING ANCIENT COSMOGONIES

I listen to the sylvan-canyoned silence of the rain
Shaping ancient cosmogonies of Venus-spinning light
Ruby-fragile echoes of eternity linger in marble-sheathed
Spaces crossing between gale-shimmering lines of arc-fated
   time,

Primeval pearl-filaments of Toledo-ethereal light
Burgeoning across vesper-palmed fields
Of Barlach-furled darkness, sable-staccato
Fountains of jasmine-crescent light surging
Through Phoenician-tempest veils of samovar-
Arching chambers, nomadic beads of auburn-molten
Light sealing porcelain pauses of time
In cormorant-subtle souls of palomar-isled,
   soft-chasmed winds,

The coral-scented loneliness of stone angels penetrates
Dusk-laminating aureoles of a divine mind
I see the plume-eeled, cinnabar-pyramid silences
Of eternity in hermetic-purple asphodels
Of amber-purifying, kelp-gyrating light.

OF IVORY-TYMPANUM SILENCES

There is a cobalt-gloaming piece of pristine-
Veiled eternity in the Hudson-spiral patch
Of forest wilderness outside my window
A chime of calypso-elixir eternity in the goldenrod-
Maned blossoms perpetuating crystalline-
Amaryllis mists of marlin-Gibraltar timelessness
Where God lingers on pastel-blue wind-helixes
Of bronze-mourning, poppy-wandering light
Where elves carve gold-mullioned
Blooms of alabaster-apostrophic light
On Berkshire-ancient texts of soft-forgotten voices
Where almond-rippling butterflies and straying souls
Of autumn deer perfect liminal truths
Of ivory-tympanum silences and
The sacred longevity of bluebell-stained time.

As Emerald-Amorphous Breezes Vanish

Only a convolvulus-astered ruin traced by Ionic-
Fading furrows where once the abbot's house stood
Now moss-distending stone burgeons in peach-dappled,
Melisma-fraying lights as emerald-amorphous breezes
Vanish into Elizabethan-soft peals and Gothic-ravined
Echoes of Penshurst-lambent dominions, Langenburg-fusing
Souls languishing at the sable-cairned edge of eternity
As moly-elliptical abysses cluster in sibyl-divergent
    perfection
A jade-misting reminder of the past, a marble-pallid
Reflection that everything animate, even Tiber-meandering
Stones, passes away in the Foscari-willowed corridors
Of dune-rusting mortality—only fragile memories
Of Einsiedeln elegance linger in the omega-shrined visions
Of the Corinthian-vaulting spirit of the Valle Crucis-
Sceptered ruin for time never separates kindred souls
And their Promethean-blossoming, diastolic-orange dreams.

Of Magenta-Vernal Hieroglyphs

An oaken-gabled line of pilaster-terraced white
Where the oleander-misting sea meets the dahlia-
Curving shore in a lilac-molding ecstasy of triadic-
Urned deluges a rosewood-tapering pastiche of madrigal-
Shearing fountains filters adamanthine-glowing sunrises
Through the portico-yellow ruins of a Tivoli-ancient
Graveyard zodiac-pale names sheltered by candelabra-
Gleaming silences saving the dead from the draconian
Vicissitudes of hourglass-sated rituals a crystal-trimmed
Sacristy of magenta-vernal hieroglyphs preserves the
     bronze-
Winding castle of the soul a Veronese-refulgent fresco
Of fleur-de-lys-concealing seeds of Polyhymnia delight
Shapes oriel-crossing masks of Caen-sutured heavens
As campanile-turquoise stained-glass pink-lunettes
Blow gently across sacred-opalescent, Ionic-looming glades.

A STONEHENGE-REDDENING RING

A Stonehenge-reddening ring of archangel-pulsing
Tulip-masques sheltering the soul in gladiolus-rising
Fountains of amaranth-tendrilled, mandarin-enthroning
Light pervading the soul in Elysian-dewed intuitions
Of asphodel-soaring, helicon-weaving eternity,
A mandala-cairned ring of ruby-gelatinous, Aeolian-
Crystalline light dissolving time in crimson-apsed,
Damask-immaculate adorations of Sargasso-silver,
Sunset-effulgent breezes shaping the andante-wandering
Soul in Tokunatsu-profound, pink-almandine breaths
Of chrysalis-golden, Tao-pristine horizon-aureoles.

A Holy-Restoring Place

Beyond the dark-fluctuating, broken-shadowed fields
Is a meadow of golden-gleaning, cirrus-manifesting light
With an old church of moss-spiring, Vatican-congealing
Stone where the sea-wind gathers tremors of eternity
And shapes them into softly tolling, maple-possessing
Silences, a dulcamara-melodic space where death
Is merely an initiation into the iris-culminating,
Artemisian-vined cyclicality of eternal life
Where the body withdraws into nothingness to let the soul
Arise in lavender-perpetual gladioli of ochre-luminous
Glory and linden-spectral Gethsemane-helixes of emerald-
Diapason light a holy-restoring place of daffodil-faithful
Blessings where the divine presence is always near,
Arles-alabaster, amaryllis-streaming stone-dances
Pulsing diamond-lintelled, magenta-frescoed horizons
Of saffron-chiming, willow-centered, Hesperus-emanating
Light in white-amber blossoms of Poseidon-wise hearts.

The Hermes-Green Silence

I am the Hermes-green silence of the auroral-mazed
Mist shaping the diamond-astered breaths of Promethean-
White clouds in lavender-gentian helixes of Tower-
Lambent timelessness I am the hydrangea-vaned silence
Of the jasmine-zephyred pond at the heart of the Rheims-
Vaulting universe shaping the amaryllis-pulsing,
Windermere-ancient mountains in adamanthine-sceptered
Veils of ruby-tendrilled light I am the amber-veined
Silence of the sunset-clouds spreading ambrosia-glistening
Lullabies of crocus-ethereal light across damask-prismed
Horizons to the hyacinth-ringed, iris-blossoming lake
At the end of the world where the Rubens-effulgent flower
Of eternity perpetuates salmon-dewed memories of
    acanthus-
Mazed dawns in almandine-leavening peals of saffron-
Astered, Aeolian-spiring light.

A Peacock-White Throne

A peacock-white throne of angels on a pink-wisteria-
Trellised stone in the amber-gleaming heart of the maple-
Rippling, Windermere-trembling cascade camellia-lavender
Voices filling the azure-diffusing glade with salmon-
Androgynous suns of Elysian-tendrilled light
A Minerva-sublime prophesy of Arbury-effulgent light
Saving cypress-angled prisms of dusk-healing timelessness
From cedar-aberrant globes of ruby-jettied, pandora-
Curving echoes as the Cyclades-petaled wind seals
    ambrosia-
Lintelled, hermetic-mullioned visions in honeysuckle-
    ringed,
Amaryllis-weaving blooms of Botticelli-scented eternity.

THE HOME OF THE WHITE PEACOCK

The Hesperus-solitary pond in the sacred glade
Is the jade-apsed eye of the lotus-germinating divine
Where the white peacock perpetuates auburn-chrysalis
Streams of Delhi-amaryllis, magenta-pellucid clouds
Across helicon-purple epitaphs of Dionysian-veined,
Mandolin-angled light

The Orpheus-mazed pond is a sapphire-pealing
Constellation of the hydrangea-gloaming luminescence
Of Arniston-protean eternity, of Venus-blue
Adumbrations of emerald-cascading light,
And of ancestral-turquoise melodies of golden-tendrilled
Breaths of acanthus-glistening light where the Eldena-
Primordial silence is a lilac-ethereal, Easter-dewed
Euphony of pink-almandine blossoms

The Hermes-lambent pond is the damask-lintelled sigh
Of the sunset-breathing, hyacinth-conceiving heart
For asphodel-effulgent eternity at the Aegean-duned edge
Of the Poseidon-cairned, phoenix-soaring horizon where
The white peacock shapes the sea in pomegranate-
    marrowed
Blooms and porcelain-astered nocturnes of the willow-
Ringed, gladiolus-weaving divine.

CORAL-ADAGIO HELIXES

Coral-adagio helixes of blue-sceptered, Vishnu-canticled
Dreams conceal archipelago-runed fantasies of lunar-
Softened light in Iliad-furtive ascensions
Of marble-globed parabola-echoes,

When the sea moves from the frosted beach
It takes an ambrosia-carved sigh of sphinx-murmuring,
Crescent-slivered silences of evening suns shattered
On sirocco-caned dirges of brandy-pearl, gaunt-pristine
    shores

When the sea moves from the hawthorne-dewed beach
It saturates moon-plasma Hebrides-soliloquies
Of latent children's laughter and onyx-bridled anemones
With oleander synergies of calico-toned shadows

When the sea moves from the twilight shore
It takes eternity along to a palomar-isled dream
Of amber-soaring epitaphs of willow-vaned light
And leviathan-blue dissolutions of carillons-fevered dawns.

IN THE BRINY-SPECTRAL DEEP

In the briny-spectral deep of alluvial-grey anemone-silences
There is a cavern where time began
Where the first rainbow-surging pulses of time
Flowed from indigo-onyx prisms of poseidon-
Tentacled, auburn-linteled coral-dreams,
A Delphic-languishing lagoon of arborealis wisdom-
    amoebae
Where time is a motionless, opal-sheathed wind
Of sapphire-helixed jonquils of light
Where time is a soft-flowing whisper of jade-
Sutured eyes of myrrh-pristine epiphytes
Where time is an Ovid-terraced memory
Of shrill-tympanum counterpanes and archipelago scansions
Of crimson-marble sunset-myths
Only eternity lingers in amber-turquoise meioses
Of Alhambra-sceptered light and pale-winnowing
    annunciations
Of hydrangea-streaming calliope-haloes,
Perpetuating zodiac resonances of Mediterranean-astral time.

THE GARDEN OF EDEN

In the turquoise-pilastered, heliotrope-vaned silence
Of the Atlas-sighing sea there is an amber-haloed,
Ruby-chastening tomb of ancient-glistening, oasis-
Sculpted flowers and auburn-madrigal light where
Adamanthine-white shapes hover ceaselessly in nepenthe-
Pallid whispers of Minerva-gentian delight, a Garden
Of Eden of marble-gelatinous, lavender-onyx vases
Of ethereal fragrances and melancholy voices
Beneath the saffron-mellifluous waves

As the evening wind ripples diamond-architraved reveries
Across mandolin-purple amplitudes the Garden of Eden
Becomes a Vertumnus-sentient, jasmine-cairned fountain
Of hyacinth-iridescent light forming the asphodel-
Lintelled heart of the sea in emerald-chastening, willow-
Veined blossoms of porcelain-tendrilled, Delphic-sated
  grace

In the hermetic-golden silence of the amaryllis-soaring,
Cyclamen-spiring sunset the Garden of Eden becomes
The maroon-crystalline destiny of gardenia-effulgent,
Primrose-sealing Atlantis as the violet-tremulous,
Albemarle-foaming waves congeal in an azure-scented
Apocalypse of sable-cresting, Dionysian-white light.

Through Larkspur-Fertile Synergies

I walk through larkspur-fertile synergies of onyx-white
Blossoms into the asphodel-burgeoning, jade-misting heart
Of the wisteria-templed universe where ruby-angled lotus-
Aureoles breathe clover-pinioned melodies of crocus-
    ascending
Light shaping the evening sea in amber-systolic memories
Of ancient-labyrinthine suns and hydrangea-fermenting
    moons
Forming the marigold-gloaming horizon in emerald-
    diastolic
Harmonies of auburn-sepulchral coronations and Rheims-
    astered
Tremors of amaryllis-inviolate eternity as the estuary-
    veined,
Magenta-rustling wind redeems the sacred longevity
Of Apollonian-ethereal groves conceiving sapphire-
    trembling
Epiphanies of cyclamen-radiant, jonquil-mazed timelessness
Along obelia-vaulting shores of London-pealing,
Primordial-golden light.

THE SILENCE OF ETERNITY

I am the emerald-vaned, yellow-opalescent silence
Of the autumn knowing that the leaves never die
Transforming themselves in the divine luminescence
Of the Church-effulgent sunset into saffron-mazed,
Wisteria-leavening petals of seraphic-liminal,
Diamond-architraved light

I am the silence of eternity
Shaping forsythia-dewed, lily-gloaming souls
Into amaryllis-helixed, iris-soaring melodies
Of Karskoe Selo-exalting timelessness
In hyacinth-deepening, asphodel-spacious groves
Of genesis-lambent, primrose-vaned light

I am the silence of autumnal synergies
Transmuting chrysalis-golden whispers and
Artemisian-lavender horizon-aureoles into the amber-
Crystalline, sapphire-astered heart of twilight eternity

I am the silence of eternity
Carving palomar-ancient, chrysanthemum-burgeoning
Rainbows of ethereal-golden, maroon-prismed light
On Cyclades-streaming reveries of orange-amethyst,
Minerva-pristine sunset-cascades.

AT THE HEART OF THE FOREST

I am the silence of the golden tree
At the heart of the forest
Whispering saffron-lyred tremors of crimson-
Helixed, hyacinth-burgeoning light across
Wisteria-trellised, Corot-lambent dreams
Of amber-pulsing, diamond-astered leaves

I am the silence of the Rheims-vaulting cemetery
Shaping ancient-lavender, meridian-cairned stones
In Psyche-altared breaths of cumulus-adumbrating,
Magenta-helicon light
In primrose-damask vortices of hydrangea-
Architraved genesis

I am the silence of the soft-forgotten, cypress-
Lintelled megaliths suffusing the evening horizon
In jonquil-vaned, jasmine-fermenting echoes
Of asphodel-blossoming, Pissarro-effulgent
Timelessness

I am the silence of the golden tree
Listening to the wind of eternity
Breathe sapphire-mazed, camellia-veined gloamings
Of Delphic-crystalline, gladiolus-soaring light
Through the pristine-hermetic amplitudes
Of the Aeolian-sibylline, autumnal-sunset grove.

An Edelweiss Castle

Ambrosia-gardens of forsythia-laden, sapphire-astered
Light scatter silver-acropolis, damask-porcelain clouds
Across soft-mitred, amaryllis-madrigal winds revealing
An edelweiss-sibylline, asphodel-burgeoning castle
Of sunset-eaved, Promethean-haloed silences where white-
Saffron petals of sirocco-mandolin repose soar
Into the afternoon haze in vernal-slender filaments
Of seraphic-murmuring light, silent menageries of virginal
Eloquence shaping phoenix-marrowed, willow-translucent
Ecstasies of amber-pealing, anemone-glistening rainbows
A castle of lilac-moist, Turner-effulgent arbors spilling
Hyacinth-andromeda diffusions of calliope-burgeoning,
Diamond-lintelled light into divine pools
Of narcissus-blossoming, sunflower-living dreams.

In the Sacred-Helixed Garden

He walks in melancholy-lambent silence
Through the marigold-gloaming garden of the elves
Where golden-sceptered stars glisten
In Lucerne-spacious pools of cypress-lavender light

He wanders through the poppy-meandering meadow
In lilac-burgeoning melodies of Calliope-leavening
Reveries as the anemone-breathing wind rustles softly
Across Chatsworth-twilight arbors of amber-wisteria light

In the sacred-helixed garden he fills his jonquil-
Effulgent soul with the asphodel-fermenting aura
Of eternity shaping the horizon in nirvana-effulgent,
Amaryllis-silver blossoms of hydrangea-streaming,
Chrysalis-ranging truths

In the primrose-latticed murmurs of the evening garden
A solstice-ringed soul carves mandolin-glazed, lotus-
Alveolar intuitions of violet-mazed, gladiolus-soaring
Eternity on pink-haloed coronations of saffron-
Conceiving, Minerva-astered light-vases.

SALISBURY-MYRRH INCANDESCENCES

I listen to Salisbury-myrrh incandescences of wind
And vernal architraves of snow-lavender light
Shape hemlock-gestating time into Fountains-solitary
Reveries of anemone-cascading, cross-latticed eternity,

I listen to orchid-misting aureoles of ancient-Chaldean
Seas and lambent-carving oracles of sphinx-surpassing
Pines redeem time on marigold-jade thresholds of
　　Schleswig-
Silver, limestone-arbored silences.

I see time congealing in a palomar-weir
Of rhododendron-stucco, apricot-tenoned light
As the wind-clover glistens talisman-white
Along the Andromeda-nape of the hyacinth-myrtle moon;

I see time in a cinnabar-quartz carafe
Of pink-setting suns and marble-olive fountain-spells
Waiting for butterfly-doves of orange-molten light
To rise in megalith-arching, Prague-blue memories
Of stained-glass, sun-dusted silences.

An Orphic Heart

Deserted silences lie about the eaves
In philomel memories of ancestral quartets
Only time is forgotten when autumn
Prayers purify the lucidity of beauty,

Three cylinders of wax-glowing light descending
From an intuitive, porcelain pause
Of elegiac-sweeping sky onto hidden covenants
Of acropolis-still corners and motionless, onyx-veiled
    pallors,

A rimless word flowing into infinity
An orphic heart converging in chrysalis-vermilion myths
Of ambivalent annunciations, returning
To a lilac-tinted hourglass.

THE VIRGIN OF THE ROCKS

Amaryllis-pink sands contemplate moist-pearl
Capricorns of Tredegar-lambent madrigals,
The virgin of the rocks suspending jonquil-jade lulls
Of time in saffron-adagio haloes of hydrangea-blue light
Shaping Stygian-architraved vagaries of time in Auvers-
Helixed, sirocco-softening whispers of seraphic-crystalline,
Chartres-acanthus repose as a solitary figure sits along
The damask-embering canal waiting for vernal-diaspora,
Sans Souci-luminous truths floating cirrus-white, pastoral-
Eglantine breaths of empyrean-diastolic sky onto camellia-
Silken petals of ethereal, pristine humanity.

Of the Poppy-Breathing Chandelier

In the heart of the pomegranate-sceptered mirror
The lavender-germinating soul can see vulcanic-sage
Reflections of the poppy-breathing chandelier
In the Florentine-astered depths of the dusk-gloaming
Mirror the saffron-iridescent, Monet-crystalline soul
Can see the birth of the laurel-architraved chandelier
In sibylline-dewed atrophies of emerald-cascading light
In the Jungfrau-spherical, mistral-gesturing chasm
The marigold-listening chandelier becomes an Aeolian-
    vaned
Lily of madrigal-turquoise feelings spreading its Janus-
Diapason wings through grail-oracular corridors
Of the universe as the sea becomes an amber-vaulting
    dream
Of Eden-liminal, Meissen-labyrinthine light.

A Silent-Solstice Figure

A silent-solstice figure gathering sophia-andante
Filaments of purple-seraphic light and pristine-
Amphora vowels of pearl-cruciform, reliquary-misting
Overtures from the crescent-aboriginal moon
To give to the divine-veiling, Aeolian-white presence
In the sacred grove of an alpine-cathedral valley
Of Lugano-red, Brahman-pealing poppies and grail-
Lavender lily-reveries, a silent-solstice figure
Shaping juniper-kinetic transubstantiations
Of moist-acanthus time in hibiscus-cascading, mandrake-
Germinating statuette-haloes of Nirvana-almandine,
Silver-architraved silences and rainbow-pulsing,
Elysian-sunset truths.

Of Elysian-Prophetic Eternity

The dance of the stars is the beginning of eternity
Stars reshaping time in magenta-solstice synergies
Of orange-diapason, autumn-musing light stars redeeming
Space in green-diffusing sails of emerald-syncopating light
Stars carving vermilion-lingering cloud-nocturnes
And pearl-gazing, horizon-articulating windmill-solitudes
On amber-misting, perpetual-mirabelle sunsets
The light of the dance is the only lodestar
Of zephyr-raising dreams and lily-helixed moons
The figures of the dance become the Venus-binding
Pilasters of Elysian-prophetic eternity
The figures of the dance are the seraphim-radiating
Seasons of violet-acanthus helicon-melodies
And the primrose-sapphire laws of Kedleston-mazed
    destiny.

Through the Moon Gate

The one who passes through the moon gate
In a gardenia-fluent perfection of fuchsia-striated light
Becomes a Shen Chou-pervading spirit of the stone-
    trellised,
Amethyst-hermetic grove where ancient-mandarin
    mysteries
Of perpetual-alabaster silences shape gloxinia-burgeoning
Tremors of emerald-discoursing diasporas in miranda-veiled
Glyphs of camellia-scented eternity where the soul
Who cherishes the rainbow-ascending fragrance of
    acanthus-
Congealing, yellow-musing, lotus-carving graces becomes
A Giverny-primordial essence of the Chatsworth-
    enchanted truth
Of the sublime-vernal soul of the celestial-prophetic,
Tiara-glistening orchid where the soul who walks across
The ruby-crenellated, Gemini-seamed bridge enters forever
Elysian-whispering, Minerva-spiring auras of dusk-
    architraved,
Pyramid-confessing immortality listening to cypress-jade,
Atlantis-radiant murmurings of acropolis-singing waterfalls
Listening to the vermilion-profound incantations of willow-
Cultivating, mandrake-dewed sages.

A Village Beyond Time

A village beyond silently massive
Auburn-duned thresholds of mist-tapering time
Beyond indigo-apertured shadows of myrrh-
Alabaster horizons suddenly appears as a saffron-
Jade shower of crystalline-autumn sunlight
Penetrates a russet-chimed Gothic spire—
A cyclamen-lingering epiphany of perpetual
Crocus-veined twilight,

A village of eternal autumns
Rises from cypress-grey cumulus-swells and pomegranate-
Haloed fields of orchid-lintelled dreams
Only a few days of chrysalis-dewed existence
In camellia-eaved mortal time
A village disappearing softly in its own eternity
A diastolic-orange reverie of moist-seamed time
A diamond-astered, emerald-altared truth
Of amaryllis-chancelled, gladiolus-architraved
Timelessness, a village shaping its immortality
In Ruisdael-pristine incantations of luminous-
Sapphire angelus-suns.

An Elysian-Petaled Cove

In an Elysian-petaled cove at the purple-sabbath edge
Of the titanic-foaming falls there is a Chamonix-hallowed
    village
Of Flensburg-lucid permanences and butterfly-mimosa
Cupolas where time, as night, passes away in the Cardiff-
Chastening radiance of philomel-auroral prophesies

A symphonic-astral oasis of Poseidon-nurtured
Silences and mercurial-jade ecstasies
Of russet-trembling, dew-glazed light
Beyond rose-engraving serpentine-mountains
And sirocco-cresting leviathan-plains

A gladiolus-converging sacristy of sapphire-
Etching dreams and Andes-aureole visions
Nestled in poppy-cloistered, turquoise-mantra
Pools of Corot-effulgent, Aeolian-lyred
Twilight

Where the inviolable-glowing shadows of evening
Cascade through peacock-discerning, narcissus-
Conceiving layers of Versailles-rippling,
Gargantuan-auburn mirrors into marble-architraved
Dawns of crimson-hermetic synchronies
And chrysanthemum-radiating, virgin-pealing solitudes.

THE SPIRIT OF THE MANSE

In the amethyst-streaming, Wynyates-enclosing mist
Of jonquil-maned, almandine-equinoctial silences
I see the spirit of the manse rise above the myriad-
Astering roofs and pink-variegated turrets becoming
A sacred space of jasmine-rolling hills and amaranth-
Dewed lawns where maple, oak, and pine blossom daily
In pristine-exalting fountains of orange-diapason,
Camellia-architraved light I am the silver-leafed,
Attingham-wise spirit of the manse shaping gardenia-
    veined chalices
Of crimson-languid melancholy into flamingo-shadowed
    trees
Of Gemini-sceptered light I am the emerald-conjuring
Spirit of amber-timeless valences suffusing the gate
Of ancient-heraldic signs with my Copenhagen-magenta,
Hibiscus-latticed dreams reshaping mimosa-lonely hearts in
    damask-
Haloed crocuses of wild-empyrean innocence

Along the hyacinth-breathing edge of the Palatine-misting
River is a grail-conceiving castle where the heliotrope-
Exalting silence of the Delphic-golden light redeems
The longevity of time where maroon-asphodel silences
Recreate the Schönbrunn-perpetual effulgence
Of willow-vaned, rainbow-acanthus love.

A CHANDELIER OF MAROON-CONTEMPLATING LIGHT

He crossed the garden of Botticelli-astral smiles
Towards the almandine-breathing light in andromeda-
    lithesome
Visions of Goya-petaled night shaping the sky in Fasanerie-
Laminating isles of adamanthine-sceptered liberty
Upon a Baroque-gesturing urn of Chagall-musing fame
Where ormolu-gentle willows turn beyond the emerald-
Germinating horizon in Biltmore-crested panoplies
Of topiary lullabies and dew-shining flames;

A trumeau-revealing chandelier of maroon-contemplating
Light in the lily-effulgent mirror of Hesperus-cadenced,
Marigold-synthetic dreams twelve Delphic-inviolable eyes
Of onyx-madrigal, Pythian-white light luring me
Into the Florentine-mazed aura of the orphic-fulfilling,
Jade-scrolled frame opening the sacred-pilastered,
    crystalline-
Acanthus fold of eternity dissolving a diastolic-meandering
Soul in Manderston-lambent effusions of silver-gleaming
    harmonies
Transforming chamomile-gentian intimations of the divine
In auburn-gloaming aureoles of odyssey-helixed epiphanies
In wisteria-oracular pulsations of amaranth-cascading,
Eroica-soaring light.

177

IN THE GREAT CHAMBER

In the Great Chamber
You don't have to worry about headstones,
Graveyards, or eulogies you can spread
Your soul out on the turquoise-paned marble
As if you were entering a Chenonceau-crystalline frieze
In the Great Chamber
You can congeal time in amber-angled vapors
Of onyx-mullioned light where the sea is a sibyl-
Wounded reverie of amaranth-templed silences
Shaping autumn-winged intuitions of eternity
On diaspora-helixed solitudes of sphinx-resolving vases
In the Great Chamber
You don't have to drink ambrosia-tinted elixirs
Or scream about the spectral frailty of a presence
Who condones perpetuities of suffering
You don't have to believe in wooden crucifixes
Or clay figurines in pastel-veneer beads
Or cranberry-glass words you can seal the Aeolian-
Gossamer tendrils of your saffron-diapason soul
In tarantella-white constellations of asphodel-pulsing,
Lily-chanting twilight.

THE GHOST AT KENILWORTH

In the gray-spindling evening the ghost at Kenilworth
Walks through the tiara-plumed, oleander-corniced portal
And the Vestal-astered priory-gate into the jade-apsed
Mists of the heliotrope-conceiving, Byzantine-furrowed
Cemetery where every grave awaits his gentle-mitred,
Hieratic-gleaming caresses where every grave knows
That he will bathe magenta-liminal helixes in the yellow-
Amaranth light of his nepenthe-linden soul
Where every spirit, recently buried or centuries old,
Feels the semblance of eternity in the cumulus-graceful
Magnanimity of his dynastic-martyred presence
The ghost at Kenilworth shares damask-pinioned globes
Of Aeolian-effusive light with diastolic-amber souls
Rising from wine-stamened, cypress-germinating pallors.

A Castle of White-Hummingbird Silences

A castle of white-hummingbird, asphodel-confessing
   silences
And purple-witnessing, pellucid-green mirrors permeates
The final edge of the iris-weaving, Sylt-vestal horizon
Where ancient-trembling cobwebs sparkle
In dusk-sated angles of omniscient darkness
Where dew-centered epodes of butterfly-amber light
Distill higher laws of Dunham Massey-vaulting eternity
A castle of silver-purifying, chrysalis-lavender silences
Surrounded by an Aeolian-hexagonal moat of pristine-
Leavening timelessness shelters empyrean-radiant, moor-
Astral breaths of solstice souls perfecting the Eden-
Ascending, lichen-globed visions and emerald-flowing
Hieroglyphs of their divinity.

IN PRIMROSE-DIASTOLIC PANOPLIES

A Warwick-refulgent castle of tabernacle-gray, ivy-
  wreathed
Silences emerges where Zarathustra-liminal lives rest
Like mosaic-pristine leaves on frost-tipped, pointillist-
Glistening marsh-staves, an emerald-lintelled,
Fyvie-gloaming castle where madrigal-almandine souls
Live forever in amaryllis-inviolate haloes, a Jacobean-
Panelled, grail-enchanting castle where the nabi-intimate,
Dawn-eglantine promises of talisman-glistening,
Amaranth-prophetic tapestries are fulfilled in vermilion-
Stamened, primrose-diastolic panoplies of hermetic-altared,
Matisse-crystalline light conceiving an auburn-vaulting
Singing-tree in the Marburg-sacred courtyard beyond ruby-
Ephemeral smiles shaping saffron-architraved melodies
Of Montacute-streaming timelessness in velvet-spinning
Murmurs of twilight-cadenced, asphodel-blossoming eyes.

OF ASTRAL-LINTELLED TIMELESSNESS

A dance of twelve amaryllis-weaving premonitions
  around an emerald-gazing dusk of Arcadian silences
A dance of twelve lily-resonant incantations
  around a mahogany-smiling, diamond-laminating
  plateau of pink-adamanthine clouds
A dance of twelve honey-breathing, rainbow-conceiving
  elves around a harpsichord-oval grove of apricot-
  mazed, arborealis-tympani melodies
A dance of twelve alabaster-jade leaves around
  an ancient-Phidian, silmarillion-valed oak-paradise
A dance of twelve burgundy-angled organ tones
  around an orange-amethyst, frankincense-nightingale
  altar
A dance of twelve poinsettia-soaring seagulls
  around a moist-carving memory of dune-victorious,
  Salome-transposing nocturnes
A dance of twelve saffron-juniper, Klee-dreaming rays
  of flamingo-gloaming, Tintoretto-distending light
  around a Chiddingstone-reigning oasis of sapphire-
  hermetic, marigold-dawning timelessness
I am the Chartres-conceiving soul of the crepuscular-
  lambent, Het Loo-orange light of astral-lintelled,
  crimson-onyx timelessness healing apocalypse-scented
  soliloquies of Elysian-dewed hearts in Goldau-
  immaculate, andante-chrysalis euphonies of mandrake-
  flaming, Bernini-soaring light.

THE FIRST CYCLE OF MORTALITY

In the molten-spherical odyssey of calico-angled
Mortality I shape twelve lives of onyx-lavender,
Marble-gesturing vastness refining the thirteenth
Ephemeral dimension as the perennially immortal self
In the first cycle I reshape primrose-blossoming,
Emerald-duned Dionysian-melodies in Arcadian-sunset
Megaliths of amaranth-diastolic, West Wycombe-
   crystalline light
I transform dusk-sated, Istanbul-damask
Murals of iris-gyrating, ivy-trellised reflections
In jade-perfecting vales of Eden-liminal,
Aeolian-swelling mirrors
I reveal sophia-marigold silences of anemone-
Purifying light along the Wessex-prismed threshold
Of a crimson-lambent empyrean-lake sheltering
Ancient-lingering, mandrake-gloaming souls
I carve millennial-silicon, rainbow-dewed contours
Of the divine on amaryllis-hexagonal eaves of diamond-
Lintelled winds and kithara-chancelled tremors of silver-
Compassionate, Penrhyn-cerulean souls redeeming
The nirvana-purple timelessness of the saffron-
Diapason inner self.

In a Timeless Vale

An asphodel-paned, lavender-cullised house
Of bronze-germinating light in a timeless vale
Unseen by mortal eyes where time is only
An echo in the pristine-suffusing radiance
Of Easter-pink clouds, where time is
Only a fleeting breath on the soft-eternal
Innocence of Vermeer-immaculate light,
Where time is only a refraction of coronal-
Turquoise space in seagull-empyrean murmurs
Of the grain-latticed, Vedic-arborealis wind,
A Saltram-luminous, cathedral-sheaved house
Where I live forever in hermetic-autumn aureoles
Of helicon-conceiving pine-sceptered light
Sealing saffron-exulting memories of orchid-
Veiling, Gethsemane-moist dreams in Uffizi-shaping
Frescoes of golden-astered, sacred-liminal light.

A Sacred-Liminal Well

I distill marigold-prophetic, apocalyptic-astral mirrors
Of amethyst-diastolic, psalm-evolving light
From amaryllis-unicorn veils of sable-ewered darkness,
I fold crocus-altared vestiges of Tintern-engraving
Time in calliope-pealing, symphonic-astral blooms
Of chrysalis-autumn moons as the zodiac-
Permeating wind carves Glastonbury-moist emblems
Of Mycenaean-kylix light on a cobalt-globed baptistery
Hovering over Thrasemine-eaved pools of ancient-
Votive, iris-misting silences—a sacred-liminal well
Healing the wounds of mortality in wisteria-
Trellised, orange-diapason ripples of zinnia-exulting,
Linderhof-crystalline light.

THE CARETAKER OF TIME'S GARDEN

Along the edge of the abyss
He climbed into the sable-gesturing, jade-
Angled mists of the granite-cased, white-
Rustling waterfall where the castle of time
Lingers in ancient-rubied shadows of primordial-
Duned eternity, among fir-sceptered boughs
Of cypress-almondine light he wove moss-amber
Filigrees of syrinx-galed time into a Rhine-dusk
Constellation of Eleusinian-legato petals,
Among autumn-tendering, tempest-softened calligraphies
Of Tudor-pealing, gentian-pulsing light he revived
Lavender-gypsum, acacia-voyaging voices of jasmine-
Crystalline, albatross-veined cairns and glacial-white,
Lichen-arching loch-souls in spacious-crenellated,
Cosmic-marble epiphanies of jonquil-diffusing,
Nirvana-sealing wisdom, he became the silent-honored
Caretaker of time's garden with its own astral-deepening,
Rainbow-enclosing, grail-ascending, apocalypse-
Spanning beauty, in consecrating himself to shape
The garden in lily-cascading, poppy-germinating frescoes
Of celestial-Florentine, amaranth-perfecting light
He endowed himself with the sage-sublime aura of eternity
The hierophant-soft, ichor-burgeoning inner light
Of eternity radiating across hermetic harmonies
Of aster-mazed, thrush-murmuring horizons
Of damask-lavender, Aeolian-dewed light.

A CASTLE BY THE SEA

There is a candelabra-gloaming castle by the twilight sea
Where time is only an apse-scented tremor of Melpomene-
Eglantine light where Sistine-azure harp-murmurs shape
Sibylline-vaulting reflections of turquoise-coronal space
In Giverny-effulgent waves of saffron-adamanthine light
Weaving Eden-liminal, poppy-breathing dreams
Along the Amsterdam-tempest shore,
There is a Tudor-luminescent castle by the evening sea
Where one never grows old watching the Dogana-pink
    frailty
Of grey-cullised time behind porcelain-silver panes
Of salmon-sheaved, Ruisdael-glowing light listening
To astral-labyrinthine omens of the ancient-prophetic wind
Fill the sky with Fountains-tremulous voices of rosette-
Ivory melancholy and apocalypse-ringed, fern-creased
Mirabelles of pearl-shadowed, Persephone-lambent echoes,
A Neuschwanstein-spacious castle of onyx-anemone, pine-
    sceptered
Solitudes where silent-solstice, heliotrope-revealing souls
Carve dove-abiding margins of lavender-architraved genesis
On coronal-magenta rainbows of diamond-immaculate
    cloud-
Synergies sealing purple-asphodel silences of sapphire-
Incarnating lilies in Elysian-lambent, almandine-hermetic
Epiphanies of Apollonian-sage, sunflower-exalting light.

AFTERWORD

I have never met Hugo Walter in person. We live on separate coasts, swim, so to speak, in separate schools. I don't know the color of his eyes or what kind of car he drives or if he even drives a car. We correspond a bit and speak on the phone, but our letters are brief and to the point, and our conversations are cordial and businesslike. I don't know the man Hugo Walter at all. I know only one thing about his personal life: he writes poetry.

On the other hand, I know the poet Hugo Walter well. I have had the pleasure of publishing six previous collections of his work (this omnibus gathering of selected poems makes seven). And I will say this: in the twenty years that I have been publishing poetry, by poets of all stripes (iamb-fettered neoformalists to free-verse liberationists, classicists and romantics, moralists, feminists, doggerelists, catalysts, you name it), I have never come across another poet like the recognizable and yet unclassifiable Hugo Walter.

I once made the statement that Hugo Walter has reinvented the color wheel of the English language. What does this mean, exactly? If you've read the book in your hands, you know. If you've skipped to the back before reading the poems, I won't tell you what it means.

One gets the feeling that Hugo Walter sees life not through a microscope or a telescope, but through a kaleidoscope. He is a poet for whom impressionism is carried to the extreme: the impressions are not created by images. Rather, the images are created by impressions, the clash of juxtaposition. The technique may not be easily explained, but one thing is certain: it is original, it is unique to one poet, and that poet is Hugo Walter.

Walter's poems do indeed stand alone among poetry. Typical of his poems (though not exclusive to Walter himself) are the vibrant splashes of color, the driving meters, and the whirlpool of lush images. Even more striking are Walter's references to a shared, pan-national human culture that mixes Greeks with Orientals, the Renaissance with the Old Testament, and the art of Egypt with the paintings of Impressionism. But what is truly ground-breaking is Walter's highly developed word-play, a creative association of concepts that, by its very audacity, differentiates itself not only by quantity but in quality: Walter has invented a new style of poetry all his own. This is poetry that knows its own vocabulary, works in its own grammar, and has its own idea of syntax. In fact, it is not too much to say that Walter has invented a new poetic language. The purpose of this new language is to explore new frontiers of understanding: with his trademark style of hyphenating odd couples of beauty, Walter combines sensual visual images with concepts and interpolates references to antiquity from all ages and all human cultures, putting layer upon layer of thought and feeling, juxtaposing nature with art, music with base nouns.

Certainly if there is any message to the poems of Hugo Walter, the message must be found with you, the reader. Whatever you glean from these coined words, you can't help but be impressed by their impressionism, can't help reeling in response to the inventive use of linguistic skyrockets by this master of romantic imagery.

—J. M. DANIEL